The Nordic Model

ms Trine Rogg Korsvik
ms Ane Stø

Published by the Feminist Group Ottar, 2013

Cover photography: The International Women's Day demonstration in Copenhagen, 2009
Photography: Mads Eskesen
Editorial secretary: Asta Beate Håland
Translation by Maria Kvilhaug, Hansina Djurhuus, Fazeela Jiwa, Guri Istad, and Tom Bechtle
Any comments or questions regarding this book can be directed to the Feminist Group Ottar at:
styret.ottar@gmail.com
The publication of this book has been made possible by financial support from the Norwegian
Office of Children, Equality, and Integration.
ISBN: 1494435373
ISBN 13: 9781494435370

Contents

Introduction

Trine Rogg Korsvik and Ane Stø

Feminist movements across the world have been calling for the abolition of prostitution since the 19th century. The demand was a logical extension of the anti-slavery campaign of that century, which was based on the conviction that no human being ought to be merchandise. But the view of prostitution as tantamount to slavery has not been held exclusively by radical feminist activists. Since its 1949 *Convention for the Suppression of the Traffic in Persons and of the Exploitation of the Prostitution of Others*, the United Nations has stated that prostitution is "incompatible with the dignity and worth of the human person and endangers the welfare of the individual, the family and the community."[1] In 1979, the UN Women's Convention stated that prostitution amounts to violence against women, a statement that was repeated in the Beijing Statement of 1995 and the Palermo Protocol of 2000.

Finding the means by which to abolish prostitution has nevertheless been a challenge. Whereas in some countries only pimping—profiting from others' prostitution—is illegal, other countries have outlawed prostitution as such, a practice that frequently leads to the persecution of prostitutes through arrest and police harassment. In both cases the sex purchasers ("johns" or "punters") go free. Thus, when feminist activists in the late 1970s came up with the idea that the johns should be the ones prosecuted for their abuse of women and children in vulnerable situations, the concept was seen as a radical proposal.

---

[1] *Convention for the Suppression of the Traffic in Persons and of the Exploitation of the Prostitution of Others*. United Nations, Office of the High Commission for Human Rights. http://www.ohchr.org/EN/ProfessionalInterest/Pages/TrafficInPersons.aspx

The demand to criminalise the johns was a consequence of the new feminist movement of the 1970s. Issues such as sexuality, which until then had been considered private, were politicised and interpreted in terms of the unequal power relationship between men and women. Feminists pointed out how prostitution historically has been one of the most conspicuous symbols of women's subordination to men. They defined prostitution as violence against women—not only against those directly involved, but against *all* women, because the existence of prostitution means that all women potentially are salable commodities. Feminists' understanding of women's subordinate position to men's as a product of both patriarchal and economic structures—not from nature or as an inevitable destiny—resulted in a conviction that the subordination of women could be changed by political means. One such means of abolishing prostitution is the legal prosecution of the johns. Feminists' attention to the johns (generally an anonymous group) implies that they are viewed as abusers and the perpetuators of the prostitution trade who enforce the enduring status of prostitutes as victims of violence.

In 1999, the Swedish Parliament, in the first such action taken by any nation, approved a law that banned the purchase of sex. A decade later, similar laws were passed in Norway and Iceland. What has come to be known as the *Nordic model* clearly states that the most numerous group in the prostitution trade, namely the johns, is responsible for criminal acts of exploitation. Though they have no illusions about the power of this law to put an end to prostitution entirely, the supporters of the prohibition against buying sex see it as a normative law aiming to change attitudes and to reduce the demand for prostitution.

The notion of a Nordic model is, however, somewhat misleading, as Finland in 2006 passed an ineffective law that prohibits the buying of sex from victims of trafficking only, while Danish law still protects the johns from criminal prosecution. In Denmark, as in countries such as France, Ireland, and the UK, the battle still rages between feminist abolitionists and those defending the status quo—namely, an unregulated prostitution industry.[2]

---

[2] In France, a large majority of the National Assembly voted in favour of a sex purchase act December 4, 2013. At the time of publishing this book, we do not know when the act will be passed to the Senate.

The legislative reforms criminalising the johns did not come easily and were the result of decades of political struggle by feminist activists in the Nordic countries. In this book, some of them share their experiences of this long-lasting, tough fight. The authors represent different segments of the feminist movement: grassroots activists, social workers, and politicians. All have been active in the campaign to amend the law in order to establish that women and children's bodies should not be commodities.

This is not a scholarly book aiming to present a balanced analysis of the prostitution debate. Quite the contrary, by giving voice to activists themselves and their personal—and highly subjective—accounts of their political experiences, we seek to document feminist actions over the past decades in this matter. This anthology can thus be read as a study in social movement activism. Besides offering empirical facts about a remarkably persistent political struggle, we hope the book will inspire activists who campaign for the abolition of prostitution and exploitation.

Outline of the anthology

This anthology was originally published in Norway in 2010 and translated into English as *The Nordic Approach* in 2011. Apart from changing the title, we have added two more chapters. Further, major revisions have been made to this introductory chapter to make it more comprehensible to readers outside the Nordic region. The whole book has also undergone a thorough proofreading to weed out the Scandinavian flaws of the first edition.

The authors come from different parts of the Nordic region. Norwegian activists are admittedly overrepresented, simply because the editors live in Norway and have actively participated in local campaigns against prostitution. Unfortunately, Finland is not represented with a chapter in this anthology because the Finnish feminist movement has, to some degree, taken part in the co-operative Nordic effort to promote a law that criminalises the purchase of sexual services. On the other hand, we are proud to present the Irish activist Rachel Moran, prostitution survivor, activist in SPACE (Survivors of Prostitution-Abuse Calling for Enlightenment), and author of *Paid For* (2013).

In Chapter 1, "The Swedish Law, *Kvinnofrid*," Anna Jutterdal, a Swedish social worker in the Prostitution Unit in Stockholm, writes about the political process before and after the enactment of the 1999 law that prohibited the purchase of sex. That law was part of the "Women's Peace Act" (*Kvinnofridslagen*), which was the result of a massive effort among feminist researchers, politicians, and lawyers to map social factors that prevented gender equality in Sweden. They argued that violence against women—especially sexual violence—is the greatest obstacle to complete freedom and self-realisation for women. In addition to banning the purchase of sexual services, the law contained a stronger rape clause and a new safeguard against sexual harassment.

Chapters 2–6 deal with the Norwegian struggle to abolish prostitution. In Chapter 2, "A Grassroots Story," activists Asta Håland and Ane Stø of the Feminist Group Ottar (*Kvinnegruppa Ottar*) write about their campaign against pornography and prostitution in Norway for the last 30 years from a grassroots perspective. They emphasise how the fight against prostitution was a logical continuation of the battle against pornography that, in the early 1980s, enlisted thousands of activists from a variety of political milieus. However, different views on sexualised oppression served to create internal divisions in the feminist movement in Norway during the 1990s.

Chapter 3, "'Things Are Not Always as They Seem,'" deals with the prostitution debates in Norway during the first part of the 21st century. Anne Kalvig, former activist in the Women's Front (*Kvinnefronten*) and now an activist in the Feminist Group Ottar, discusses the rhetoric of NGOs that appears to be working to help prostitutes and johns. Based on public debates in which she has participated, Kalvig's chapter argues that through their resistance to understanding prostitution as violence against women, these NGOs, as well as some gender researchers, in fact legitimise prostitution. In order to avoid the "victimisation" of prostitutes, these state-funded actors depict prostitution as a free choice and as "work" that actually may be rather glamorous.

After the breakup of the Soviet Union in 1991, the borders were opened up to people and trade. The dark side of the fall of communism was that the economic collapse had forced many Russian women into prostitution. During the 1990s, the northern part of Norway experienced a dramatic surge in the prostitution industry. The effect was particularly noticeable in the small village of Tana in Finnmark County, which was inhabited in large part by indigenous Sami people. In Chapter 3, "Johns and Activists in the Sami Area," Sami feminist activist Marit Smuk Solbakk tells the story of a tough battle against pimps and johns in a small village where everybody knows each other. Tana became an important symbol because the damage that prostitution causes became apparent, and it was observed how the normalisation of prostitution turned a vast number of local men into johns. Simultaneously, Tana became a symbol of how campaigning for the abolition of prostitution actually yields results.

The debates about viewing prostitution as violence against women have also taken place within the women's shelter movement. In Chapter 5, "'Radical Feminists' and the Dispute About How to Understand Prostitution," Tove Smaadahl, the leader of the Secretariat of the Crisis Centres (Norway's main agency for women's shelters) explains the political development within this movement regarding prostitution since the 1980s. She recounts the establishment of the Network Against Prostitution and Trafficking in Women in 2002 and shares her experiences in the RRSA Project, a relief measure for female victims of trafficking set up by the Secretariat of the Crisis Centres in 2005.[3]

The legal prohibition against the purchase of sexual services was approved by the Norwegian Parliament in 2008. In Chapter 6, "The Campaign Within a Governmental Party," Kirsti Bergstø, a member of the Central Board of the Socialist Left Party (*Sosialistisk Venstreparti*, or SV), writes about the discussions concerning this matter within this political party. Although SV is a proclaimed feminist and socialist party, leading politicians were reluctant to support the proposed law, originally put forward by the party's youth organisation, of which Bergstø was the leader. Bergstø and her associates finally won the battle at the National Conference in 2007, thus ensuring a political majority for this act in Parliament.

---

[3] RRSA: Re-establishment, Organising safe places to stay, Security, Assistance.

From Norway we move on to Iceland. In Chapter 7, "The Fight to Criminalise the Purchase of Sexual Favours: An Icelandic Fighting Saga," Kolbrún Halldórsdottir, former Minister of Environmental Protection and Nordic Minister of Cooperation of the Left-Green Movement (*Vinstrihreyfingin—grænt framboð*), writes about the political process that preceded the resolution to penalise the purchase of sexual services in 2009. The act was initiated by women's organisations—with the women's shelter organisation Stígamót in the lead—and by female members of Parliament. Midway through the financial crisis, they succeeded in gaining a majority in favour of this proposal. The following year, on March 23, 2010, they also gained a majority in favour of the penalising of strip clubs, where most of the prostitution had been taking place.

As in other Nordic countries, leftist political parties in Denmark have approved programs that promote a legal prohibition against the purchase of sex. However, to date (2013) the liberal and conservative majority in the Danish Parliament has blocked a decision similar to that of Sweden, Norway, and Iceland. In Chapter 8, "Take a Stand, Man!" Hanne Helth, an activist in the 8th of March Initiative, relates how it has been necessary in Denmark to create a broad coalition in the campaign for a sex purchase ban. In that country, activists have sought alliances with different societal entities than those that have generally been sought out in the other Nordic countries, including actively drawing men into the awareness-raising campaign that targets men's violence against women.

Chapters 9 and 10 appear for the first time in this edition of the anthology. Chapter 9, "Prostitution and the Commercial Value of Youth," is written by Rachel Moran. Her personal experiences as a prostitute in Ireland from the age of 15 to 22 have formed the basis of her current courageous activism in promoting a Nordic law against prostitution in her home country. In Chapter 10, "The Crusade of the Pro-Prostitution Lobby," Ane Stø and Asta Håland analyze the debates on prostitution in the Nordic countries over the last few years, placing special emphasis on how research that is biased and poorly conducted is used to undermine the law that bans the buying of sex. The last chapter of the anthology,

The Feminist Movement

Throughout this anthology, activists from the feminist movement tell about their political experiences of fighting prostitution from various perspectives and positions. Since there seems to be some confusion regarding what the feminist movement is about, it is important to point out how we define this movement. First of all, we will highlight that we view the feminist movement as a social movement aiming to change society. With an awareness of the existence a wide range of interpretations of feminism, we will emphasise that we define feminism as a *political ideology* that views gender as the primary (although not the sole) determining influence for structuring society and everyday life. Specifically, it is an ideology that recognises the existence of a gender-specific subordination where women are systematically discriminated against, and that also questions the legitimacy of this gender order by stressing the need for collective mobilisation to confront the unfair distribution of power.[4] Those who not only accept this as true but actually *act collectively* to change the gendered power structures are here defined as activists in the feminist movement. In other words, the feminist movement is not identical to women's organisations that work to improve women's lives without challenging the established gender order.

As in other social movements (e.g., the antiracist movement and the environmental movement), the feminist movement consists of organised groups, NGOs, and independent individuals who identify with the movement. However, in our opinion, the most important resources for social movements are organised grassroots groups that are democratically managed and accessible to ordinary people. Using their own capacity and ability, these groups can offer their creativity and engagement through their influence on the political development of the organisations. This is seldom the case with professional NGOs and lobbying groups, where paid employees and experts determine the policy of the organisations. We argue that in order to understand some of the

---

[4] This definition is highly influenced by Solveig Bergman (2002): *The Politics of Feminism. Autonomous Movements in Finland and West Germany from the 1960s to the 1980s*. Abo Akademi University Press, p. 19.

conflict lines in the prostitution debates, it is important to bear in mind the distinction between democratic membership organisations and professional NGOs. As numerous examples in this book will show, the most active political figures promoting the criminalisation of johns are from democratic, grassroots organisations. On the other hand, professional NGOs, which are usually run by social workers, academics, and other "experts" claiming to speak on behalf of prostitutes, in fact rarely represent more than a handful of carefully selected prostitutes. Yet the image of NGOs is not correspondingly narrow. As we will see, in all Nordic countries shelters for women victims of violence have played a crucial role in the campaign for criminalising the johns. Still, the women's shelter movement originally sprang from the autonomous feminist movement and became professionalised only after years of voluntary solidarity work, which probably explains its openly feminist stand on the issue.

Although unaffiliated individuals may play an important role in social movements through their writing or cultural activities, or simply by joining demonstrations and discussions, the strength of democratic grassroots organisations is that they are generally able to sustain mobilisation over time. Further, in times where the general interest in feminist politics is low—or even hostile—organised groups that offer their participants a social and political milieu in which they can find joy and pride in taking part in a struggle for a common goal have the advantage of creating an internal solidarity that individual actors are deprived of. The organised groups also serve as reservoirs of knowledge and experienced activists—crucial resources for renewed mobilisation when feminist politics again attracts attention.

Characteristics of the feminist movements in the Nordic countries
In contrast to its counterparts in countries such as the US, the UK, Germany, and The Netherlands, the feminist movement in the Nordic countries has been quite united in its demand for a legal ban on the purchase of sex. Yet the feminist movement is rather diverse in the Nordic countries treated in this anthology. What follows is a brief summary of what we consider to be typical characteristics of these movements.

In *Sweden*, the largest Nordic country (population: 9.5 million), the feminist movement is characterised, more strongly than other Nordic movements, by its division into an institutionalised section within the political parties, and a second, autonomous, radical feminist and separatist section. In *Norway* (population: 5 million), the feminist movement is more oriented toward grassroots activism than in Sweden. It has sometimes used rather strong measures in order to place sexualised oppression on the political agenda, but it has also established an alliance with feminists within the political establishment.[5] The feminist movement in *Iceland* (population: 300,000) resembles the Norwegian movement insofar as it combines grassroots activism with campaigns for institutional power. Examples are the electoral alliance known as the Women's List (*Kvennalistinn*), founded in the 1980s, and the alliance of activists and established politicians from all corners of the political landscape that brought about the sex purchase ban in 2009, as well as legal action against strip clubs in 2010. In *Denmark* (population: 5.5 million), the feminist movement has, since the 1970s, generally been more countercultural and less legalistic than in the other Nordic countries. In the 1970s, the Danish feminist movement was regarded as the strongest in the Nordic countries, but it became increasingly isolated during the 1980s. When issues concerning sexualised violence, pornography, and prostitution were put on the international feminist agenda in the late 1970s and after, the Danish movement did not take a clear position because sexual liberalism was extraordinarily strong in leftist movements. In Denmark, there were few traces of any battle for the abolition of prostitution at all before 2007, when the Danish Women's Society (established in 1871!) placed penalising the purchase of sex on its agenda.

The rather strong position that the feminist movement enjoys in the Nordic region is probably the result of a combination of its relatively small population and a democratic tradition of broad popular movements with access to institutional power.

---

[5] See Hernes, Helga Maria (1987): *Welfare state and woman power: essays in state feminism*. Oslo: Norwegian University Press.

Competing framings of prostitution

In obtaining an overview of the features of the battle for the abolition of prostitution in the Nordic countries, some analytical frameworks that draw from social movement research may be useful. Without going into the details of this huge research field with its opposing paradigms, we will sketch out some characteristics of successful social movement mobilising.[6] First, activists of social movements have to agree in their perception of reality: they must explain what the problem is all about, explain the reason why the problem exists, and identify those who are to blame. Second, they have to find solutions to the problem—deciding which strategies to use and which alliances to make. Third, they have to motivate people to mobilise in the common struggle. This mechanism is often referred to as a *framing process*. The concept of *frames* refers to how a phenomenon is explained and understood, or—to state it more figuratively—*what is in the picture*. The various ways in which a phenomenon may be framed have consequences for the proposed solutions.

To explain the analytical concept of frames, we can use the example of two typical but competing ways of framing prostitution: Prostitution as *"the world's oldest profession"* has been a persistent framing in prostitution debates for decades. This framing implies that prostitution is considered natural and thus inevitable. A logical consequence of this fatalistic understanding is that there is not much to do about it, except to improve the "working conditions" of those in the "profession." In contrast, prostitution framed as a *gender political problem* assumes that prostitution is a product of a culture in which women are subordinated to men. Since the inequalities are socially and culturally constructed, it is possible to change them through political means, such as passing laws that restrict men's customary right to control women's sexuality.

Throughout this book we will see that the battle over how prostitution is framed has been—and still is—pivotal in the debate over the ban on buying sex. Even among actors that to a greater or lesser extent

---

[6] A book that offers an easy-to-read overview of social movements is Tarrow, Sidney (1998): *Power in Movement. Social Movement and Contentious Politics.* Cambridge, UK: Cambridge University Press.

consider prostitution to be undesirable, there are several competing frames: prostitution as a social political problem, as a public order
problem, as an immigration problem, and, finally, as violence against
women.

In Chapter 2, Håland and Stø discuss the political consequences of
framing prostitution as a social problem or a gender political problem.
They show how the framing of prostitution as primarily a social problem may just as easily lead to the utopian conclusion that capitalism
has to be overthrown before prostitution can be abolished, as to cyni-
cal claims about improving the "working conditions" of the individual
prostitute. When prostitution is framed as a gender political problem—
an approach driven by an understanding that women as a group historically have been structurally and culturally subordinated to men—the
conclusion is less ambivalent and calls for concrete measures in order
to bring prostitution to an end.

Since the late 1970s, feminists have framed prostitution as violence
against women, a framing that is advanced by the authors of this book. In
Chapters 4 and 5, Solbakk and Smaadahl, respectively, discuss the resistance that this framing has met among NGOs that claim they are speaking
on behalf of prostitutes. According to the critics, framing prostitution as
violence against women deprives the prostitutes of their dignity and ability to act as subjects because they are seen as victims. The victim position
is, according to this view, automatically linked to a degrading form of passivity and helplessness. Instead, the critics prefer to frame prostitution as
a free choice that supposedly will make the prostitutes feel happier and
more active. The assumption that being a victim is automatically degrading for prostitutes and other people suffering from abuse became widespread in the 1990s. We think this is a noteworthy development insofar
as resourceful men in public debates still have no problem presenting
themselves as victims of a feminist state. It seems that the "attractive-
ness" of the victim position is closely linked to the power and resources
possessed by those advocating that position. However, when feminists
frame prostitutes as victims of violence, no intrinsic passivity on the part
of the victim is suggested. Instead, this framing implies recognition of the
abuse that prostitutes have endured and makes a statement that holds

the abuser—and not the victim—responsible for the abuse. The aim of the collective feminist mobilisation is evidently that victims of violence shall cease to be victims.

The feminist movement in the Nordic countries does not recognise the distinction between "involuntary" and "voluntary" prostitution. The term "voluntary" presupposes that human beings are free and that there are real choices. However, prostitution is "chosen" as an alternative for those who have few other options to earn a living in a patriarchal society. To frame prostitution as a free choice does not create an image of happier prostitutes; instead, it ignores the vast difference in power between the one who sells her body and the one who buys it. It is the potential john who has a real choice—to not buy sex.

The Swedish and Icelandic laws prohibiting the buying of sex clearly state that prostitution is violence against women. In contrast, the Norwegian law frames prostitution as a social problem and a public order problem. This lack of a gender political framing of the law as a means of challenging gendered power relations is probably the reason why the "effectiveness" of the law is still disputed in Norway (see Håland and Stø, Chapter 10). Although the Norwegian feminist movement won a victory when the law was passed in 2008, it was only a partial victory in terms of framing prostitution as a feminist issue. At a discursive level, the opposition was simply too strong.

Enemies and allies

For social movements to mobilise successfully, it is helpful for them to be able to identify their enemies as well as to form broad alliances. In the campaign to abolish prostitution in the Nordic countries, it has not been particularly difficult to spot the enemies. Pimps profiting from prostitution and gangsters organising trafficking of women were already considered criminals long before the current debate on criminalising the buying of sex. Identifying the johns as enemies has been somewhat more controversial, as it has been widely believed in the Nordic countries that the john is a poor guy unable to find someone to have sex with except

prostitutes.[7] Compared to many other countries, buying sex is generally seen as unacceptable in the Nordic countries, a shameful act that the
johns themselves try to hide.[8] However, research studies of johns have
unmasked the myth of the john as a pitiful, unattractive guy, and testimonies from the johns themselves reveal that the majority have partners
and that their desire to power and control women is their fundamental
motivation for buying sex. Feminist activists have certainly shared these
insights. Particularly in Norway, feminist activists have been confronting
pimps and johns directly, as shown in Chapters 2 and 3.

Nevertheless, pimps and johns are seldom the ones participating in
public debates about prostitution legislation. The opponents of amending
laws that ban the purchase of sex come from the entire spectrum of society—from politics, academia, the media, and NGOs claiming to support
prostitutes. Simultaneously, allies of feminists fighting for the abolition
of prostitution are found in the same milieus. Later we will come back to
this rather complex situation, which varies across the Nordic countries.

As mentioned above, forming broad alliances is crucial to the success of mobilisation within social movements. Allies may be found in
other social movements and among elites, as well as in the media and
among ordinary people. As several of the chapters in the book demonstrate, Nordic feminist activists have generally had a pragmatic attitude toward cooperation in the fight against prostitution. Instead of
insisting that the "right" analysis about patriarchy must be the basis

---

[7] The situation was different when prostitution was regulated during the 19th century.
In this period the johns were regarded as resourceful, healthy, and vital men, as shown
by Swedish historian Yvonne Svanström in "En själklar efterfråga? Om torskar och
sexkjöpare under hundra år." In Y. Svanström & K. Östberg (Eds.) (2004): Än män då?
Stockholm: Atlas Akademi, pp. 213–244.
[8] Whereas surveys show that 40% of Spanish men have bought sex one or more times
in their lives, the corresponding number in Scandinavia is 13–14%. See Sven-Aksel
Månsson (et al.) (2007): "Mäns könsköp—en meningsbärande handling på flere nivåer,"
in Sex säljer. Kön och makt innom prostitution och pornografi. Historical research on
sexuality has shown that there is a correspondence between sexual freedom and prostitution. In cultures where women are supposed to be virgins until marriage, for example
Catholic cultures, the level of prostitution is much higher than in countries that have a
freer attitude toward sex, such as the Nordic region. In her book Les lois de l'amour. Les
politiques de la sexualité en France (1970–1990) (Éditions Payot, 1991), Janine Mossuz-
Lavau shows how prostitution decreased dramatically during the "sexual revolution"
of the 1960s and 1970s.

for cooperation with potential allies, feminist activists have sought alliances anywhere. This pragmatism can be explained as a continuation of a Nordic tradition of broad popular movements mobilising for a common goal despite political, social, and cultural differences on other matters. A classic example is the labour movement, which historically has had a much stronger position in the Nordic region than in most other places. This movement has been crucial in the development of welfare state measures, often through pressure from the women's and feminist movements. It is worth noting that the labour movements in Denmark, Norway, and Sweden have actively supported laws banning the purchase of sex from a gender political perspective. The Nordic feminist movement's lack of sectarianism in forming broad alliances against prostitution may explain why it has been able to place the demand to ban the purchase of sex on the national political agenda.

So far we have touched on the complex situation regarding certain milieus that have contrasting opinions regarding the act that prohibits the buying of sex—a situation that has had consequences for feminist activists in forming alliances for mobilisation. In the following section, we will discuss how opinions on the matter have varied across time and across countries in the realms of party politics and academia, and within various support services for prostitutes. We will also clarify what we consider the pro-prostitution lobby, a central concept in this anthology.

The politics of political parties

A general trend in the Nordic countries is for the socialist and social democrat left, including the labour movement, to support a statutory prohibition against the buying of sex, while the political right has opposed it.[9] However, the picture is more complex. As in other countries, there are branches of the left that use various arguments to oppose the abolition of prostitution. Arguments against it may be portrayed as anarchist and/or liberalist opposition to legal regulations, embodied in the common phrase "You can't ban everything you don't like." Quasi-feminists claim that the

---

[9] In the Nordic countries, the left refers to socialists, communists, and social democrats. Non-socialist liberals can be referred to both as right wing or centre, depending on their welfare policy.

prostitute is the controlling party in prostitution transactions, using her sexuality as a tool to exploit men. Prostitution is framed as a win-win situation: the john gets sex and the prostitute earns easy money. Frequently linked to this argument is the idea that feminist abolitionists feel threatened by sexually liberated prostitutes because they represent a menace to feminists' supposedly puritan vision of sexuality. Not least, there is widespread belief that the ban on the purchase of sex worsens the situation of prostitutes (see Chapter 10). These arguments against abolitionist prostitution politics are not only promoted by leftists who lack an analysis of gendered power relations, but also by right-wing liberalists. Furthermore, there is some non-leftist support for a legal prohibition of the purchase of sex on the grounds of feminist arguments or humanist values.

On a national political level, political parties' viewpoints on the matter vary across the Nordic countries. In Sweden, the Swedish Social Democratic Party and the Left Party have for decades been champions for gender equality, at times predating the grassroots movements. As shown in Chapter 1, all Swedish parties from across the political spectrum currently support the prohibition of buying sexual services. In Norway, the political situation is different. On a national level, right-wing parties are still opposed to the act, though there are exceptions on the local level. However, the Norwegian Christian Democratic Party was the first to support a law forbidding the buying of sex. Later, the socialist Red Party and the agrarian Centre Party followed. In 2007, a majority in the Norwegian Labour Party, as well as in the Socialist Left Party, supported a legal sex purchase ban (see Chapter 6). In both parties the leadership opposed this, and the approval resulted from successful grassroots mobilisation. In Norway, the Liberal Party has been the most consistent opponent of penalising the buying of sex, and it speaks from a liberalist standpoint about the free choice of the individual.

In both Iceland and Denmark, the dividing line moves along the right-left axis, though in Iceland (as shown in Chapter 7) women from various political parties brought up the matter. In Denmark it took a long time for the lines of political division to show. Here the Socialist People's Party was the first to support a sex purchase ban, followed by the Red-Green

Alliance and, in September 2009, the Social Democrats (see Chapter 8). Despite the fact that surveys show that many members of the non-leftist parties support this proposed law, these parties maintain a liberalist attitude toward prostitution. After the parliamentary election of September 2011, a new leftist government was formed. However, the Minister of Justice from the Social Democrats has actively worked against implementation of the law, and parties opposing the sex purchase ban retain their parliamentary majority, so no such law has yet been approved.

Academia

Research on prostitution reflects the diversity of framings that were discussed above and, not unexpectedly, shows an amazing variety in the conclusions—both across the Nordic countries and across time. Whereas feminist scholars in Sweden contributed to a large extent to research that laid the ground for the Swedish Sex Purchase Act in 1999, scholars in Norway and Denmark have taken different positions.

In Norway, feminist researchers were among the first—if not actually the first—to demand the penalising of johns. As described in Chapter 2, criminologists Cecilie Høigård and sociologist Liv Finstad combined research and social work to help women and children escape from prostitution. In their 1986 book *Backstreets—About Prostitution, Money and Love*, they proposed penalising the purchase of sex.[10] However, this opinion did not last long among researchers. In 1989, sociologist Annick Prieur and criminologist Arnhild Taksdal published the book *To Put a Price on Women: Men Who Buy Sex*, in which they rejected the proposal to penalise sex buyers and claimed that the goal must be to engage in a dialogue with the johns.[11] Since then, many Norwegian researchers have actively opposed the sex purchase ban (see Chapter 10).

---

[10] Finstad, Liv & Cecilie Høigård (1986): *Bakgater: om prostitusjon, penger og kjærlighet*. Oslo: Pax. Finstad had already forwarded this demand in 1981 after she had run the so-called Oslo Project to help child prostitutes. See Finstad, Liv, Lita Fougner, and Vivi-Lill Holter (1981): "Oslo-prosjektet. Erfaringer fra to års forsøksarbeid blant barne—og ungdomsprostituerte i Oslo 1979–1981." Barnevernskontoret i Oslo, 28 September 1981, and Finstad, Liv, Lita Fougner, and Vivi-Lill Holter (1982): *Prostitusjon i Oslo*. Oslo: Pax Forlag.

[11] Prieur, Annick, & Arnhild Taksdal (1989): Å sette pris på kvinner: menn som kjøper sex. Oslo: Pax.

Scholars from Denmark have distanced themselves from the limit imposed on free choice that a sex purchase ban implies. But even here there are researchers such as Kennet Reinicke, who researches masculinity, who move against the current. As Hanne Helth shows in Chapter 8, Reinicke has distinguished himself as a spokesman against the idea that buying sex is a human right to which men are entitled.

Academia is political in terms of both what is being researched and what is *not* being researched. Nordic research on prostitution shows little interest in the damage to the health of prostitutes, traumas that persist over time, or the consequences of prostitution for relatives and friends, to name just a few issues. Nor is there any research being conducted on what might stop men from buying sex, or how to help men who wish to stop this behaviour.

Support Services for Prostitutes

An interesting difference between the various prostitution debates in the Nordic countries is the position taken by support services. In Sweden and Denmark, support services for prostitutes have backed social measures that may discourage prostitution and have pushed eagerly for both public education campaigns about the realities of prostitution and a legal sex purchase ban. The Swedish Church City Mission (*Stadsmissionen*), Procentrum, and the Prostitution Unit, as well as the Danish The Nest (*Reden*) and the Prostitution Competence Centre, aim to help as many people as possible out of prostitution and to prevent recruitment. In Iceland, the support system for prostitutes has been largely run by the women's shelter Stígamót, which has played an important role in the campaign to penalise the purchase of sexual services.

In Norway, NGOs providing support services for prostitutes have been divided over this question. In 2008, the Salvation Army, for example, took part for the first time in history in an International Women's Day 8th of March demonstration in which the main slogan was "Penalise the johns now!" As described by Smaadahl in Chapter 5, the Crisis Centre Secretariat has also fought for a change in the legal act. In contrast, the publicly funded Pro Centre, which is both a relief measure for prostitutes and a "national centre of expertise with responsibility for everything that has to do with prostitution,"[12] has established itself as a powerful opponent to the sex purchase ban. According to Kalvig in Chapter 3, the general attitude of the Pro Centre is that a woman in prostitution must be respected first and foremost as someone who makes a choice and must in no way be seen as a victim.

The Pro-Prostitution Lobby

In this book you will read a great deal about the pro-prostitution lobby, also called the pro-lobby. But what is the pro-lobby? The pro-lobby operates openly within the UN, the EU, and other international institutions that attempt to persuade politicians to legalise prostitution. They have succeeded in countries such as The Netherlands, Germany, and New Zealand. They have also succeeded in coercing the UN into labelling prostitutes "sex workers," a discursive trick signalling that prostitution is a choice of work like any other.[13] The pro-lobby is represented by the TAMPEP International Foundation, an EU-financed project that aims to legalise prostitution in Europe in the guise of advocating "human and civil rights of female and transgender migrant sex workers."[14]

The methods and arguments of the pro-prostitution lobby are repeated from country to country. They show up at meetings on prostitution in order to prevent abolitionist resolutions, and they infiltrate political parties and organisations.[15] They cynically take advantage of prostitutes to advance their legalising agenda; they claim that only "happy hookers" are entitled to an opinion on the question of prostitution.

In Sweden, the pro-prostitution lobby emerged immediately after the passage of the Sex Purchase Act in 1999, in the form of the NGO ROSEA, The National Organisation for Sex and Erotic Workers (*Riksorganisationen för sex- og erotikarbetare*). The organisation became inactive sometime during the early part of the 2000s but was

---

[12] As stated on the Pro Centre website, http://www.prosenteret.no/
[13] "UNAIDS Editors' Notes for Authors," UNAIDS, 2006
[14] See the TAMPEP (European Network for HIV/STI Prevention and Health Promotion Among Migrant Sex Workers) website, http://tampep.eu/
[15] They use "heckling" to disrupt meetings and rallies where the aim is to fight prostitution. Ironically, this method was invented by the British suffragettes in their fight for women's right to vote.

followed by SANS, the Swedish Coalition of Sex Sellers and Allies (*Sexsäljares och allierades nätverk i Sverige*). As its name indicates, non-prostitute allies who also want to abolish the Sex Purchase Act have been included in this group. In Denmark, the Sexworkers' Interest Group (*Sexarbeijdernes Interesseorganisation*, or SIO) emerged five days after the 8th of March Initiative had begun its campaign for a sex purchase ban in 2007. With help from a group of sexologists, psychologists, media personalities, and johns, SIO has since become a media favourite.

In Norway, the pro-lobby is represented by PION, the Prostitutes' Interest Organisation, and the above-mentioned Pro Centre. PION was established by social workers back in 1990, and despite the name, it has never organised prostitutes, a group on whose behalf it claims to speak.[16] Apart from offering juridical counselling and distributing condoms to prevent AIDS, state-funded PION's main activity is promoting the legalisation of prostitution in public debates. The Pro Centre was established in 1983 to assist prostitutes, and has for many years been headed by the social worker Liv Jessen, TAMPEP's coordinator in Norway.[17] Several of the chapters in this book refer to Jessen as an important opponent in the debates since she—with the help of the media—has had a great influence over the framing of prostitution in Norway. As an "expert," she has used her position to legitimise prostitution as well as to attack feminist abolitionists.

Successful organising

Although the pro-prostitution lobby is powerful, this anthology documents how feminist activists in the Nordic countries have succeeded in framing prostitution as a gender political question that has resulted in legislation that penalises sex buyers in Sweden (1999), Norway (2008), and Iceland (2009). The authors tell stories of years of struggle over how prostitution should be framed and resisted. The stories are dramatic and bear witness to how feminist activists have been verbally attacked, ridiculed, harassed, and threatened. But it is also a story of

---

[16] See the PION webpage, http://www.pion-norge.no/
[17] See the TAMPEP website, http://tampep.eu/

successful political mobilising. What lessons can be drawn from this mobilising?

As discussed above, it is crucial to identify one's enemies and to form broad alliances. Furthermore, the importance of strategic planning, organising, and hard work must be recognised. Patience and the determination not to give up despite rigorous opposition have been decisive activist virtues. In addition, a wide range of political actions has been employed, including public demonstrations, public meetings, distribution of flyers in the neighbourhood, setting up websites, lobbying with politicians, and direct action against brothels and johns. Also of great importance are the infinite number of letters to the editor that have been written, as well as posts on various Internet discussion sites.

The importance of visibility in public debates cannot be underestimated, although feminist actions against prostitution frequently are criticised in public. An illustrative example is when activists from the Feminist Group Ottar in 2003 tacked up posters all over the central part of the capital, Oslo, depicting the prime minister and other prominent male politicians as johns. The action was harshly criticised but brought a lot of media attention. Ottar activists were interviewed by major media and were thus able to communicate their opinions on prostitution. Such forms of rude and disruptive action may be effective for activists whose cause is ignored by the media. Moreover, they form the basis for heroic stories to be shared in the activist community and serve to create internal solidarity, thus inspiring further actions. Nonetheless, long-term mobilising and alliances with elites are indispensable to implementing legislative reforms.

A failed reform?

Throughout Europe, the media have brimmed with stories about how the Nordic model that penalises the purchase of sex has failed. After Sweden passed the Sex Purchase Act, the Norwegian Parliament was paid frequent visits from Swedish "sex workers" who talked about how dangerous it had become to prostitute oneself in Sweden. A similar Scandinavian exchange was observed after Norway passed the law that penalised buying sex, with actors from the Pro Centre telling the Danes that the Norwegian ban was not working. However, the numbers recorded by the very same centre tell a different story: prostitution has decreased, and considerably so.

The Sex Purchase Act has contributed to a reduction in the number of johns. As the Swedish criminal law expert Madeleine Leijonhufvod has pointed out, an important shift in attitude has occurred among young Swedish men. Simply put, they no longer think that it is acceptable to buy sex. Seventy percent of the Swedish population supports the ban, substantiating its important preventive effect.[18] This illustrates the power that this legal act has to change the attitude that prostitution is inevitable or legitimate.

The evolution of positions taken by the police is noteworthy. In all Nordic countries, the police were initially sceptical about the Sex Purchase Act. The Swedish police, however, have actively promoted the law and certainly influenced the Norwegian police when the latter decided to support the proposal in 2006–2007. In both Sweden and Norway, the police are now steady supporters, because the act gives them increased latitude in the battle against human trafficking. Even in Denmark there is movement among the ranks of the police.

Although the Sex Purchase Act is working, there are still flaws in the prostitution policies of Norway and Sweden. In both countries the support measures fail to follow up with the prostitutes. In Norway, this is partly because of a lack of government commitment, and partly because the Pro Centre does not have the ambition to help women out of prostitution. In Sweden, the authorities followed up the law with public awareness campaigns to prevent men from becoming johns, notably through a national campaign in schools. The Norwegian Ministry responsible for gender equality has still not shown any inclination to launch such preventive projects—which, as mentioned earlier, may

---

[18] *Prostitution i Norden,* Nordisk Ministerråd, 2008, p. 362. A recent report from Sweden confirms that the sex purchase ban is still supported by most Swedes, and that the number of johns has continued to decrease. Svedin, Carl Göran, Linda Jonsson, Cecilia Kjellgren, Gisela Priebe, & Ingrid Åkerman (2012): *Prostitution i Sverige. Huvudrapport. Kartläggning och utvärdering av prostitutionsgruppernas insatser samt erfarenheter och attityder i befolkningen.* Linköping University Electronic Press. Available at http://prosentret.no/wp-content/uploads/2013/07/Prostitusjon-i-Sverige.pdf

be due to the fact that the framing of prostitution as a gender political problem not has garnered sufficient acceptance.

According to the authors of this anthology, prostitutes who wish to leave prostitution need to receive far more support than they do today. The necessary follow-up must, among other things, recognise that a prostitute has been the victim of abuse and thus has a right to rehabilitation in the form of financial reparation as well as therapy to treat the traumatic effects of a life in prostitution. If victims of trafficking wish to return home, they must be given a residence permit and a promise of essential social services in their own countries. Just as prostitution is not a form of aid from wealthy men to underprivileged women, a prohibition against buying sex is not a measure to serve the interests of immigration policies.

This anthology documents the fact that feminist liberation struggle actually works. The feminist movement in the Nordic countries has put forth political demands to transform society into a better place for women and children. Compared to other countries, women in the Nordic countries have achieved a relatively high degree of economic independence and political power. That political power has been used by women to acquire enhanced rights and to limit men's violence against women, and the Sex Purchase Act is an expression of this. As optimistic feminists, we believe it is possible to change the attitudes and actions of human beings. With this in mind, we want to express our great gratitude to the contributors of this anthology and to those who partake in changing the world through a tireless fight for the rights of women.

The Swedish Law, *Kvinnofrid*: Knowledge About Men's Violence Against Women

Anna Jutterdal

The point of departure for this chapter is my personal work as secretary of information and my temporary position as the leader of the Prostitution Unit in Stockholm.[19] In my work I have acquired knowledge about Swedish politics in this area. I have taken part in the ongoing debates among individual politicians, intellectuals, and scientists. Most important, I have been able to access the stories of people who sell or have sold sexual services and of people who buy sexual services.

This chapter explores the political climate in Sweden during the 2000s vis-à-vis prostitution and human trafficking. It also touches on discussions about prostitution that take place from time to time in the public debate in Sweden. Neoliberals promote the view that prostitution is like any other profession—that is, a form of work—while those with whom the Prostitution Unit in Stockholm works relate how angry and offended they feel at hearing such arguments. For these people, life can be totally consumed with finding strategies that enable them to survive while selling their bodies to other people.

---

[19] The Stockholm Prostitution Unit is a municipal unit within the Social Services and the Labour Market Administration of the City of Stockholm, working with persons regardless of gender or sexual orientation who buy or sell sexual services or are victims of human trafficking for sexual purposes. The unit works in outreach, offers conversational support and medical counselling, and informs/educates about prostitution and human trafficking for sexual purposes. For more information: www.stockholm.se/prostitutionsenheten

Naturally, the Swedish Sex Purchase Act was introduced, which in Sweden (as opposed to Norway) is seen as a tool for achieving equality between women and men. The Sex Purchase Act, which was passed in 1999, was part of a package of laws that addressed men's violence against women. In Sweden, the legal sex purchase ban thus developed for different reasons than it did in Norway. In Sweden, debaters, politicians, and scientists had long advanced the argument that prostitution was a structural expression of men's superiority as a group over women as a group. Just as feminists during the 1990s succeeded in shedding light on the fact that "domestic violence" is usually about *men's* violence against women, they now succeeded through the passage of the Sex Purchase Act to shift the focus to the demand for prostitutes. That is, they brought to light the long-hidden aspect of prostitution—that those who purchase sexual services are men.

In this relatively short chapter, which is tasked with describing the political climate and the debate on prostitution in Sweden, an exhaustive study is impossible. However, an attempt will be made to paint a picture that includes both politics and the experiences of people who prostitute themselves.

Swedish Politics in the 2000s
The parties of the Swedish Parliament all agree that prostitution and human trafficking must be fought. Whether they are right- or left-wing parties, this is an area of politics in which they all agree. However, there are certain differences in what the various parties emphasise. The left is clear about prostitution being an expression of a structural gendered power imbalance and sees prostitution as a manifestation of men's violence against women, while the conservative side emphasises the harmful effect of prostitution on the individuals involved. But during periods of both conservative and left-wing governments in Sweden during the 2000s, the agenda has been the abolition of prostitution and human trafficking for sexual purposes. Common to both conservative and left-wing governments is the understanding that there is a *demand*—after all, without buyers there would be no such transactions. Disregarding

the political bent of the government, one also understands prostitution as an obstacle to equality between women and men.

In Sweden, prostitution and human trafficking for sexual purposes share common ground. Even if the actions and punishments vary between the two, they are still considered to be connected and dependent on one another. The experiences of the Swedish social services agencies and the police—who, in their work, come into contact with people who buy and sell sexual services—show that it is very difficult to keep the two types of prostitution separate. For example, it is only after the social services personnel talk with the people who sell sexual services on the street, or after extensive police surveillance and subsequent action, that we know if a case involves prostitution or human trafficking for sexual purposes.

Local Activities, but a National Concern

In Sweden, individual municipalities have considerable autonomy, which means that it is up to each municipality to decide how the campaign against prostitution and human trafficking should be organised. In Sweden's three largest cities—Göteborg, Malmö, and Stockholm—there have been for many years municipal units that have worked with people who prostitute themselves. During the last decade, these units have even begun to work with those who purchase sexual services. Since these are municipal activities that are not statutory, not all units work in the same way, and they have different levels of financial resources at their disposal. In contrast to Norway, Sweden has no national centre like the Pro Centre in Oslo, which works with people who prostitute themselves or with victims of human trafficking for sexual purposes.

For a number of years, the National Social Administration has been responsible for the governmental task of following up on the Sex Purchase Act and gathering knowledge about the development of prostitution. The establishment of a national clearinghouse of expertise on prostitution and human trafficking for sexual purposes is a necessary step toward strengthening the effort both on a national and a local level. Today, the knowledge is spread among various professional groups, voluntary organisations, and scientists who come into contact with prostitution and human trafficking for sexual purposes. A national centre would provide invaluable support for the three municipal prostitution units in the big cities regarding the development of methods that would facilitate a quicker and more effective way of discovering new trends within prostitution and the effectiveness of our efforts, among other things.

The Origins of the Swedish Sex Purchase Act

In the early 1990s, Sweden's second government report on prostitution was presented.[20] Among other things, the report proposed that buyers as well as sellers of sexual services should be penalised. However, the majority of organisations and institutions that were asked to comment on the report were critical of the proposal, and it was rejected. Instead, the Swedish Sex Purchase Act is built on the *kvinnofrid*[21] proposition that was put forth in 1998 by the social democratic government. The introductory lines of the document state: "The proposition presents measures to counter violence against women, prostitution and sexual harassment in the workplace."[22] Criminalising the johns was a very radical move, and many countries found the Swedish action incomprehensible. However, the law was enacted against the backdrop of a series of legal proposals with the common purpose of mitigating men's physical and sexual violence against women and providing a stronger legal position to women who are exposed to violence and children who witness domestic violence. In other words, the Sex Purchase Act was passed in the context of equality measures.

Since 2005, when the law was strengthened, it has been called the Purchase of Sexual Services Act (*Lagen om köp av sexuell tjänst*) and reads: "Those who achieve a casual sexual relation by means of compensation are penalised for the purchase of sexual services with fines or imprisonment up to six months."[23] "Compensation" refers to the act in which a person pays money to someone for sexual services,

---

[20] The first was *Prostitutionen i Sverige [Prostitution in Sweden]* SOU 1977:01, and the second was *1993 års prostitutionsutredning [Prostitution Report of 1993]* SOU 1995:17.
[21] *Kvinnofrid* = "Women's Peace"—a legislative package based on extensive studies of violence by men against women, and whose purpose was combating it and thus achieving a higher level of equality between women and men.
[22] The Government's Proposition 1997/98:55 Kvinnofrid:55.
[23] 6 kap. 11 § brottsbalken.

or when a person gives something else in exchange for sexual services. Unlike the Norwegian Sex Purchase Act, which includes the purchase of sex abroad, the Swedish Sex Purchase Act covers only the purchase of sex in Sweden. During the years 1999–2008, 702 persons were brought to court for the purchase of sexual services in Sweden.[24]

Today there is general political agreement about the Sex Purchase Act, and there are very few individual liberal politicians who are critical of the sex purchase ban. At the time of this writing, a government report was being undertaken with the purpose of analysing the sex purchase ban from a legal perspective. The report was presented in April 2010. Some politicians have expressed a desire to strengthen the Sex Purchase Act regarding punishment levels and believe that the law, just as in Norway, should include the purchase of sex abroad.

In 2002, two years after the UN passed the Palermo Protocol, the first law was passed in Sweden dealing with human trafficking for sexual purposes. Since 2004, the crime of human trafficking has included trafficking that does not transcend national borders. Whether a person buys sexual services from a person who, in the legal sense, has been exposed to human trafficking, or from a person who prostitutes her/himself, the john may be prosecuted according to the legal sex purchase ban. Since 2003, 12 people have been charged with human trafficking.[25] It is difficult to obtain the conviction of a suspected perpetrator of human trafficking because the circumstances must be such that the victim had no other option than to submit to the perpetrator's will. Only then is it regarded as human trafficking. In some cases that bear a similarity to human trafficking, the perpetrator may be charged with pimping rather than for human trafficking. Even the law on human trafficking offences is about to be reconsidered.

The Extent of Prostitution in Sweden

It is difficult to calculate the extent of prostitution in Sweden, and the existing estimates of the number of clients are quite outdated.

---

[24] Brå, Brottsforebyggande rapport 2008: *Sexuell människohandel—En fråga om tillgång och etterfrågan. [Sexual trade in human beings—a question of accessibility and demand]*: Stockholm, Brottsförebyggande rådet.
[25] Brå, Brottsförebyggande rådet, statistik.

A survey of Swedish sexual habits that was published by the People's Health Institute[26] in 1999 shows that about 12% of men who responded to the survey had at some point purchased sexual services in Sweden or abroad.[27]

Regarding the number of people who sell sexual services, the Social Authorities in 2007 estimated that the number of people involved in street prostitution was about 200 in Stockholm, fewer than 70 in Malmö, and around 30 in Göteborg.[28] Generally speaking, street prostitution has decreased in these three big cities in the last 10 years. It could well be that the legal sex purchase ban has had the desired effect—that is, it has discouraged potential buyers. Another possibility is that making contact for the purpose of buying sex now takes place to a greater extent on the Internet rather than on the street.

In Stockholm, street prostitution has decreased by one-third in about 10 years. The Prostitution Unit in Stockholm estimates that over the last couple of years, about 180 persons sold sex per year in street prostitution.[29] Also in Stockholm, the number of drug-addicted females who prostitute themselves on the street has decreased; in fact, hardly any heroin-addicted women can be found on the streets today, whereas in Malmö it is common that women who prostitute themselves on the street are also drug abusers. Regarding people who offer sexual services on websites, the Social Authorities in 2007 estimated their number at 304 persons. Of these, 57 were males.[30] Exact numbers of women sold within human trafficking for sexual purposes in Sweden are not known. However, estimates from the National Police Authorities from 2004 showed that between 400 and 600 women are transported to Sweden every year to be exploited in prostitution.[31]

---

[26] "Folkhälsoinstitutet."
[27] Folkhälsoinstitutet 1999, *Sex i Sverige, om sexualitet i Sverige 1996 [Sex in Sweden, about sexuality in Sweden 1996]*, Stockholm; Folkhälsoinstitutet.
[28] Socialstyrelsen 2008, *Kännedom om prostitution [Knowledge about prostitution]*. Stockholm: Socialstyrelsen.
[29] Stockholms stad 2009, *24 frågor och svar om prostitution [24 questions and answers about prostitution]*. http://Stockholm.se/prostitutionsenheten/
[30] Socialstyrelsen 2008; *Kännedom om prostitution*. Stockholm: Socialstyrelsen.
[31] RKPs: Rapport 2004:2. Stockholm: Rikspolisstyrelsen.

Prostitution also occurs among LGBT (lesbians, gays, bisexuals, and transgendered) people, but less is known about that form of prostitution. RFSL, the Swedish Federation for Lesbian, Gay, Bisexual, and Transgender Rights,[32] has taken upon itself the governmental task of investigating the extent of the trade and the situation of LGBT people who buy or sell sexual services.

Prostitution in the Public Debate

Many tend to associate the word prostitution only with prostituted women. This is not surprising, since it is exactly those women who sell sexual services who have historically been the objects of society's restrictive measures. Their clients, who are closely linked to them in practice, remain hidden from the public.

In many cases, suspicion has flourished that highly regarded male politicians, industrialists, and civil servants have been involved in the purchase of sexual services from women. The most famous example is perhaps the Geijer scandal of the 1970s, in which prominent males— politicians, major corporate leaders, cultural celebrities, and others— were suspected of having bought sex in Stockholm at a brothel that was well known at the time. No one knows what really happened, or perhaps the lid was slammed shut on the truth. Though it was not a crime at the time to buy or attempt to buy sexual services, no one ever came forward with the truth.

Since the passage of the Swedish Sex Purchase Act, the debate on prostitution has become more public. Previously, conventional wisdom was that weird and slightly unusual men buy sex on dark backstreets. The act has helped us to see that the picture drawn earlier by prostitutes was correct all along: all sorts of men buy sexual services. Through criminalisation, the buyers have been forced into public view, and only recently the police have been able to show that even well-established men buy sex from women.

---

[32] Riksförbundet för homosexuellas, bisexuellas och transpersoners rättigheter, formerly Riksförbundet för sexuellt likaberättigande.

Debates about Prostitution

While the various parliamentary parties agree that prostitution and human trafficking must be fought, debates among intellectuals, academics, activists, and some individual politicians take place at regular intervals. Alongside the national policy, these debates reveal various views about prostitution and the Sex Purchase Act in particular. Often there are neoliberals who promote views about removing the legal ban; feminists, on the other hand, are protective of the legislation. One would think the arguments are new, but a closer look shows them to be more than 100 years old.

Neoliberals argue for the legalisation of sex purchasing in exactly the same way liberals did in the early 1900s.[33] Then, as now, the intention was that prostitutes should have better lives and that the state should not interfere when two adult people want to buy or sell sexual services. They believe that the Sex Purchase Act leads to more violence against prostitutes and that they are thereby more vulnerable now than before the act became law. There are academics who propose that prostitution is just like any other work or profession.[34] Driving this line of argument seems to be a wish for prostituted women not to be stigmatised by society, among other things.

However, Swedish society's view on prostitutes was despicable long before the Sex Purchase Act was passed. During the 19th century, there was a so-called "regulation"[35] that made sure the state had control over prostituted women. In those days, prostitutes were accused of spreading sexually transmitted diseases. One also regarded prostitutes as loose women who led men to depravity. It was thus not the Sex Purchase Act that led to the stigmatising of prostituted women.

---

[33] Svanström, Yvonne, 2006: *Offentliga kvinnor: prostitution i Sverige 1812–1918 [Public Women: Prostitution in Sweden 1812–1918]* Stockholm: Ordfront.

[34] Dodillet, Susanne, 2009: *Är sex arbete? Svensk och tysk prostitutionspolitik sedan 1970-talet. [Is Sex Work? Swedish and German Prostitution Politics since the 1970s]*: Vertigo.

[35] The "Regulation" is the title of a system that, in the late 1800s, forced prostitutes to receive medical attention on a regular basis with the purpose of reining in the spread of sexual diseases. Sex purchasers were not forced to submit to the same kind of medical screening.

Another positive outcome of the Sex Purchase Act is that many prostitutes indicate that it has become easier to report maltreatment and abuse to the police, something that they avoided earlier, for fear of being met with disrespect because they prostituted themselves. Now that it is the johns who are the criminals, it feels easier for many to report abuse. It has also proven easier for many to seek help in order to stop selling sex, because the Sex Purchase Ban makes it clear that it is not the prostitutes who are doing anything illegal.

Those who argue for the legalisation of sex purchases from the position that selling sexual services is like any other work argue from an individual perspective in the sense that they rarely seem to consider power relations in society. Feminists promote views that highlight the norms and attitudes of society regarding women and men, masculinity and femininity. Many feminists believe that there are discriminatory norms that lead to women and men being regarded in different ways when it comes to, for example, sexual desire. An old and much too common opinion is that men have a greater sexual drive than women, an idea that easily leads to opinions such as "women should partake in sex even if they do not want sex," or that it is good that there are prostitutes so that men who do not get sex any other way can get it from them. This image of men's sexuality, in which men are reduced to slaves of their bodily desires, is grotesque.

My opinion is the same as that of many other feminists, namely, that men as a group have more power than women as a group. Abolishing the Sex Purchase Act would not lead to a more equal society and would not promote better lives or less stigma for women (and men) who live in prostitution. Rather, the present Sex Purchase Act should be sharpened to discourage more buyers. The level of punishment for an offence reflects how serious the state considers that offence to be. Today, the punishment for the purchase of sex is on the same level as that for petty thievery, an equivalence that is unreasonable. It is also important to modify the Sex Purchase Act so that people who prostitute themselves are considered victims of a criminal offence in the eyes of the law. This would lead to prostitutes being able to apply for compensation for damage.

Paving the Way

Feminists have paved the way for both greater sexual freedom for women and for the Sex Purchase Act. Toward the end of the 19th century, feminists and other free thinkers fought for the rights of prostitutes by campaigning to abolish laws that regulated the prostitutes but not the pimps and johns. They have campaigned to help women out of prostitution. And feminists, activists, and politicians who support equality have campaigned for the passage of the Sex Purchase Act.

The social consequences of the fact that women and men throughout history have had sex outside of the norms of society and the laws governing sexual relationships have always had a greater impact on women than on men. Until the 1860s, sexual relations outside of marriage were illegal. Women who had children outside of marriage were considered whores.[36] The feminist movements of the 1900s that lobbied for contraceptives, legal abortion, and women's right to their own bodies and sexualities, among other goals, paved the way for greater sexual freedoms for women today. Still, even today women are judged according to the ancient binary of "madonna or whore," depending on how she has sex, with whom and how many partners she has sex with, or even just based on rumours about her. Though it is possible for women today to have multiple sex partners without always being stigmatised as bad women, it still cannot be said that society treats women's sexuality in the same way that it treats men's. A man can have many sex partners without being considered a bad man, and the idea that men's sexual desire is greater than women's lives on. Even today, there are those who suggest that men go to prostitutes because they do not get enough sex from their wives, or because they are single. According to this antiquated belief, the prostitute *must* exist—for men and their sexual needs.

With today's greater freedom regarding sex and sexuality, it is also possible to criticise old truths. One old truth is the assumption that selling sex is something women are forced to do. What if it is the case, as neoliberals claim, that women want to have sex in this way, often

---

[36] Svanström, Olsson, Hanna, 2006: *Från manlig rättighet till lagbrott—Prostitutionsfrågan i Sverige under 30 år. [From male right to criminal offence—The Question of Prostitution in Sweden during 30 years.]* Kvinnovetenskaplig tidskrift no. 4, 2006.

and for monetary compensation? We are back where we were in 1900, back to an individualistic perspective and a discussion about choice. Of course there are women who voluntarily prostitute themselves. But based on the tales of prostitutes that we encounter at the Prostitution Unit in Stockholm, we get the picture that an overwhelming majority of the women who prostitute themselves would never have begun if they had perceived an alternative.

Neoliberals often seem to wed themselves to the idea that prostitution is about sexual desire. They argue that society should not interfere if adults want to buy sex, because this is just one of many ways to have sex. If adult people want to have sex in an arrangement wherein one is paying and the other receives payment, then that is just as acceptable as when a heterosexual couple has sex at home in their bedroom. And in some sort of utopian society where all people have equal power, where women, men, blacks, whites, heterosexuals, homosexuals, and bisexuals are equals—that is, where no oppression exists—that would be fine. But we are not there. For me, this is not a way of saying that certain forms of sex are wrong. But as long as there are groups of people who have more power and resources than other groups, as long as society values individuals differently based on gender and sexuality, I think that it is very dangerous to argue as if no power relations existed. The experience I have in my work at the Prostitution Unit tells me that the majority of the people who sell sexual services do it for reasons other than sexual desire. And for me it is self-evident that society must assume the responsibility of supporting all of those who have suffered in prostitution.

According to neoliberals, it is easy to see a clear division between people who live in Sweden who prostitute themselves and people who are the victims of human trafficking for sexual purposes and who prostitute themselves in Sweden. Prostituted Swedish citizens are thus viewed as a group who have chosen to sell sex, as if it were any other profession, while only those that have become victims of human trafficking are forced into prostitution. Naturally, women who are trafficked in order to sell sex are in many ways more vulnerable and are trapped in a situation similar to the slave trade. However, this does not imply that women in "ordinary" prostitution are not suffering or that they would have chosen prostitution if they had had other opportunities.

The Johns—Men of Many Faces

This is how johns are described in a report on human trafficking that was published by the Counsel for Preventing Crimes.[37] The johns, too, are a heterogeneous group. They are just as bashful as those who sell sexual services. My interpretation is that many men who purchase sex from women have more to lose than what is commonly suspected. Many of the buyers are, as mentioned above, well established in society; they have families, jobs, and a secure financial situation.[38] At the three Prostitution Units, johns, too, are offered support to stop buying sex. In Göteborg, the unit has worked for more than 10 years with people who want help in order to stop purchasing sexual services. There have been talk therapy programs for johns in Malmö and Stockholm over the last few years. The buyers that the Prostitution Unit in Stockholm have met are people—until recently strictly men—who want to stop buying sex. An insight that I have developed about johns that has been invaluable to me is that the men who attend talk therapy at the Prostitution Unit do not seem to have oppressive views of women. There are surely johns who do, but it is good to know that not all do. It sheds light on the fact that the explanation of structural societal inequality may not be directly translatable into action on the individual level.

The Responsibility of Society

Prostitution is an explosive matter that concerns a woman's right to her own sexuality, gender inequality, norms about the sexuality of both genders, sexual morality, shame, and, finally, power.

As we participate in important discussions about prostitution, there is a reality in which all too many women (and men) are suffering from the selling of sexual services. These are the people that society

---

[37] "Brottsförebyggande rådet," Brå, Rapport 2008: 24.
[38] Brå, Rapport 2008:24; Stockholms stad 2009, *Prostitutionsenheten verksamheter och kunskaper [The Prostitution Unit—Activities and Knowledge]*, www.stockholm.se/prostitutionsenheten

has a responsibility to support. Prostitutes with whom we work at the Prostitution Unit in Stockholm tell us they get angry and feel offended when they hear arguments such as "selling sex is the equal of any kind of profession." For all the people who prostitute themselves or who have prostituted themselves and suffered in prostitution, it becomes wholly unimportant to ponder what exactly makes it so loaded to sell sexual services compared to selling other services. For people with prostitution experience, the reality is often about developing strategies in order to handle the memories of selling sexual services and their bodies to other people. It could be about basic matters such as facilitating everyday life, and many times it is also about the need to process difficult experiences. What all these people have in common is that they carry a lived experience—prostitution—in a society where men as a group still have more power and more freedom than women as a group, and where prostituted women are still stigmatised. For all these women (and men), it is important that society continue to offer relief measures that exceed what is being offered now.

Epilogue

In Sweden we have a bad habit of thumping our chests and proclaiming our own superiority. But when it comes to the Sex Purchase Act, I cannot resist. I offer thanks to all the feminists who paved the way for that parliamentary resolution! It was a courageous Parliament that passed the act 10 years ago, and it is with pleasure that I note how more countries have copied Sweden in regard to this question. Norway was first, followed by Iceland in the spring of 2009. In Denmark, discussions are ongoing about passing a Sex Purchase Act. That more countries understand the importance of a Sex Purchase Act is invaluable.

The Sex Purchase Act, like all legislation that acts as a counterweight to women's vulnerability, is not something we should take for granted. Such laws need to be guarded always, and we must be ready to defend them. With this knowledge in our pockets, it is fantastic that more countries have adopted their own versions of the Swedish Sex Purchase Act.

A Grassroots Story

Asta Håland and Ane Stø

On Thursday, November 20, 2008, at around 10 in the evening, cheering broke out in the Norwegian Parliament gallery among 30 feminist activists. They had just witnessed an historic event: the law that penalises the purchase of sexual services had been passed by Parliament. Since 2009, Norway has implemented a one-sided penalty on sex buyers, the second country in the world to do so after Sweden.

Campaigning for women's rights has never been easy, but in certain periods, rage and collective efforts have resulted in such a powerful movement that it has succeeded in obtaining the power to establish definitions. It happened in the last century during the struggle for women's right to vote. It happened during the 1960s and 1970s in connection with the women's campaign for the right to work and for abortion. By the middle of the 1990s, this second wave had receded. Authorities and international organisations no longer saw a need to prioritise a change in power relations between men and women.[39] In Norway, many were of the opinion that equality between women and men had gone far enough, or even that it had gone too far. Some demanded giving cash support to mothers so that they could stay at home with children. The global pornography and prostitution industry was advancing powerfully and had acquired the power to influence legislation in country after country. In the legalised trade of humans in many parts of the world,

---

[39] For example, the last time the Nordic Counsel arranged the Nordic Forum for Women's Politics was in 1994. The following year was the last in which the UN arranged a women's conference.

they were now given access to new commodities, since the fall of the Soviet Union created millions of new poor people from Eastern Europe.

In Northern Europe, we experienced a huge increase in the spread of pornography both in the private and in the public arenas: commercials and other media were increasingly influenced by pornography, and we saw an explosive rise in the trading of women. In Norway, feminist resistance to this development immediately escalated. Throughout the 1980s, we had had demonstrations across the country against mud wrestling, strip shows, and wet t-shirt contests. The resistance declined around 1990, but the struggle continued throughout the decade. A new opponent in the battle for women's liberation appeared when H&M papered the whole country of Norway with underwear commercials that were strongly influenced by pornography. These posters were so eagerly torn down that H&M sometimes experienced a shortage of posters to wage the same campaign in Sweden. This line of resistance enjoyed great public support, in part because feminist groups had been organising against the porn industry ever since the first "porn bonfire" flared in Oslo in 1977.

The Flaming Porn Bonfires
The goal of the porn bonfires was to halt the expansion of pornography. The fight acquired clout when the Norwegian broadcasting network made a documentary in 1982 featuring anti-porn activists from the Feminist Women's Front (Kvinnefronten). The documentary had a huge impact on public opinion, and not long after, the Joint Action Against Porn and Prostitution[40] emerged. At the peak of their power, the Joint Action had the support of many hundreds of thousands of people. In addition to the Women's Front and other feminist activists, organisations such as the YWCA-YMCA,[41] the Norwegian Society of Rural Women, and the Housewives' Association claimed collective membership.

This took place just after the great victory of the feminist movement in Norway: the right to self-determined abortion, a law that was passed in 1978. The transition from the abortion campaign to the

---

[40] Fellesaksjonen mot porno og prostitusjon.
[41] KFUM, KFUK.

anti-pornography campaign was dramatic in many ways. The recognition of female sexuality was an important part of the abortion campaign, and in this area the Church was a great opponent. However, in the anti-pornography campaign we were suddenly allies. This speaks to the political maturity and courage of both the feminist movement and the Church.

There were several radical leftist intellectuals who disapproved of this alliance. They considered all nudity—even pornography—a form of rebellion against the Church, Puritanism, and a conservative, old-fashioned Norway. Many were veterans of the liberal student rebellions of the 1960s and 1970s whose slogan, "Make Love, Not War," was very popular, and free love was an ideal. The feminist movement as a whole was also influenced by the battle against Puritanism: we threw away our bras, sunbathed topless, and nursed our babies in public spaces. But unlike the radical intellectuals, the Norwegian feminist movement did not consider porn and prostitution to be expressions of the sexual liberation that we had fought for during the abortion campaign. Porn against porn—the use of public displays of pornographic images with comments and analysis— was soon a recurring event at schools, meeting halls, and military camps. Throughout Norway, public meetings, petitions, and demonstrations were organised; countless letters to newspaper were written; and shop owners were asked to remove porn from their shelves. (A great many shop owners actually did that.) The great coalition of different women's organisations together managed to halt the liberalisation of the legislation on pornography that characterised our neighbouring countries. The movement, therefore, was not at all unified on all issues; it included feminist activists, radical intellectuals, anti-Puritans and Christian Puritans, socialist cadres, researchers, and social workers. In the first years, when the power of the movement was great and its success indisputable, the ideological contradictions were not so easy to spot.

Different Approaches Divide
Again, the Joint Action Against Porn and Prostitution of the 1980s included organisations and activists with somewhat conflicting political and religious views. They could, however, agree on the understanding

of porn and prostitution as abuse of poor women who lacked other options. This social-political critique of the sex industry emphasised why women ended up in prostitution, and how they could be helped out of it most effectively. Researchers, activists, and authors succeeded in changing society's view of prostitutes from being regarded as antisocial outcasts to victims of a failed social policy.

In 1986, the feminist researchers Liv Finstad and Cecilie Høigaard published a ground-breaking book on prostitution.[42] The book is a qualitative study of prostitution based on in-depth interviews with prostitutes, pimps, and johns, and presents stories of sexual abuse during childhood, failure of parental care, drug abuse and poverty, and—not least of all—the repeated sexual abuse that prostitutes suffer during prostitution. The most startling aspect, though, is the book's emphasis on the sex buyers (a group that, until then, had been left completely out of every prostitution debate) and its conclusion highlighting the necessity of criminalising the johns. The emphasis on the johns indicated a new understanding of prostitution, as feminists argued that prostitution ought not to be understood only in terms of social politics but within the frame of gender polices where men have the power to buy women's bodies. In order to bring the sex buyers to light, many actions were instigated against them. The most famous one was spray-painting the term "john" on the cars of men who were trying to buy sex.

However, with the new focus on johns and the demand that they ought to be penalised, the movement started to break down. A social-political understanding of prostitution may promote arguments both for the criminalising of the johns and for the improvement of the conditions of the women in prostitution. The advantage of such a social-political approach is that it does not require any advanced political understanding, just empathy, and thus is easy to agree on. For many social workers and politicians, however, it is an easy transition from a compassionate social-political view to a liberalist standpoint of "respecting individual choice."

---

[42] Liv Finstad, Cecilie Høigaard (1986) *Bakgater—Om prostitusjon, penger og kjærlighet*. The English translation, *Backstreets—About Prostitution, Money and Love*, was published in 1992.

As a result of the great coalition against porn and prostitution, the Pro Centre was established in 1983 as the primary relief measure for prostitutes. The feminist movement and the relief system worked together to help prostitutes out of prostitution, to combat the prostitution industry, and to change societal attitudes. Academics and social workers could explain how pornography and prostitution affected the victims as well as society as a whole. But for some of these advocates, especially among the social workers, the perspective of the individual soon overshadowed the collective and societal viewpoint. For these people, the most important thing was to protect the interests of the individual porn model and prostitute rather than to protect the society against porn and prostitution and prevent recruitment into the industry. Under that kind of understanding, the intersection of gender, power, and society are irrelevant; it is the worth of the individual that matters. Individuals in prostitution should be protected against abuse in their way of life, but not protected from the way of life itself.

During the 1980s, the contradictions between the social-political and gender-political understanding of prostitution became more obvious. Street actions in which feminist activists painted "john" on the cars of sex buyers were questioned, and the publication of names and pictures of abusers and johns was a much-debated tactic. The criticism came from two directions: representatives of the social-political perspective thought that such actions were harmful to prostitutes as it hindered the trade, while some members of the left thought that exposing the johns would sharpen gender differences and thus weaken the class struggle. But those who participated in the controversial actions also received a great deal of support, both for their methods and for their political message.

Within the feminist movement of the late 1980s, there was much discussion about the slogan "Fight Porn and Prostitution." Some thought it too negative and too Puritan and succeeded in changing it to "No to Porn, Yes to Erotica." In 1989, the central board of the Women's Front, which until then had been the leader in the campaign against porn, became influenced by so-called "sex-positive feminism," which embraced "feminist porn."

The board of the Women's Front dissociated themselves from the alliance with traditionally popular organisations, and Puritanism and the Christians were again defined as the main enemy. Demonstrations against porn and prostitution were considered expressions of Puritanism and even as abuse of the women in the sex industry.

This schism in the Women's Front was highlighted in 1989 when activists from the organisation's local division in Stavanger created the exhibition "Pornography and Myths." Here we showed porn to inform people about the contempt for women that pornography spreads; that is, we used the "porn-against-porn" method. The central board of the Women's Front tried to stop this exhibition when it was about to embark on its tour of other Norwegian towns. Its argument was that the porn-against-porn method harmed the models. It was argued that since the models had already appeared in porn magazines, we should not expose them further. At the very least, the central board argued, one should try to hide the identity of these women by censor marking their eyes. Our side argued that the eyes reflected how the models were really feeling about their condition. The debate about censor marking, from our point of view, spoke to the basis of our political work: is our goal charity or solidarity? Are we fighting on behalf of "the others"? Are we to help "the weak ones" by making their lives easier with condoms and lube? Or is porn and prostitution a question that affects all of us and has to be fought on a societal basis?

In the Women's Front, we lost the debate about censor marking and thus lost our focus on solidarity. The charity perspective became dominant. Prostitution was no longer seen as a matter of general interest but was defined as a separate phenomenon with no connection to pornography. The individual prostitutes became the sole object of attention. With such an understanding, it became difficult to see the interconnection of patriarchy, men, and society in prostitution.

Parts of the political left sympathised with the social-political perspective and contributed to creating a public space for prostitutes to come forth with soppy stories and ask for support and respect as "sex workers." This perspective created fertile ground for the growth of a pro-prostitution lobby in Norway. Toward the end of the 1980s, the pro-prostitution lobby tried to redefine the political project from a fight against prostitution to a campaign to improve conditions within prostitution. Since the end of the 1980s, parts of the Norwegian support services system for prostitutes have been working as an integrated part of the pro-prostitution lobby against measures that may limit the prostitution industry. Together with PION, The Prostitutes' Interest Group (Prostituertes Interesseorganisasjon I Norge), the Pro Centre, and parts of the Church City Mission (Kirkens Bymisjon) have formed an unofficial coalition that has actively supported the position that Norwegian legislation should legalise prostitution, and inserted themselves into the discussion of normalising prostitution and portraying it as harmless in the public debate.

PION was founded in October 1990 by social workers affiliated with the Church City Mission and the Pro Centre, along with a handful of prostitutes. The purpose of the organisation was to "show both the good and the bad sides of working as a prostitute," according to its information flyer. The "harmless" idea that prostitutes were to be heard in public debate had, even from the start, an authoritarian tone: No one may offer an opinion about prostitution who is not personally involved in it! The first spokesperson of PION, a social worker, explained in newspaper interviews and articles that she had been wrong in assuming that prostitutes were emotionally damaged.[43]

The dispute about porn and prostitution came to a head at the National Congress of the Women's Front in January 1991. Before the dramatic split, the Women's Front included both the women who started PION and those of us who were to start the Feminist Group Ottar (Kvinnegruppa Ottar). By forming this new organisation we got rid of the internal contradictions and could finally concentrate on the struggle against porn and prostitution. What remained of the Women's Front continued to expend much energy on internal and external disputes about the politics of porn and prostitution.

While the feminist movement was devoting its energy to internal battles, brothels and topless bars were cropping up in Oslo. Prostitution

---

[43] *Klassekampen*, June 22, 1991.

increased across the country, especially in the phone-sex and in door markets, while H&M occupied the public space with pornified commercials on enormous boards. A weakened feminist movement did not have the strength to counter all of these attacks. The Feminist Group Ottar was created just a month after the split in the Women's Front in 1991, but the price of division was high. The remains of the Women's Front and the new Feminist Group Ottar combined were a much smaller group of people than the whole organisation had been before. The Joint Action Against Porn and Prostitution—that is, the broad coalition of large popular organisations and feminist activists—died in the process.

In the fall of 1992, activists from the feminist movement and the unions gathered for demonstrations outside the newly opened strip clubs. After a couple of months of weekly protests, the demonstrations reached a climax when the Oslo police used horses to clear away demonstrators who had blocked the entrance of a go-go bar. The brutal behaviour of the police engendered great sympathy for the demonstrators. A commercial bureau offered a free ad campaign in which angry women were encouraged to send in used bras to the Minister of Social Affairs as a protest against topless serving. The minister received 36,000 used bras from all over the country. The number of bras speaks volumes about the resistance to the liberalist development. Many people contacted the Feminist Group Ottar to seek our assistance in getting rid of the neighbourhood brothel or the local strip club. For our organisation, the early 1990s was a period of countless actions and demonstrations against brothels, wet t-shirt contests, mud wrestling, stripping, and topless serving.

The Individual Perspective Wins Acceptance

Regardless of the broad public agreement that prostitution was a societal problem, the individual perspective steadily won acceptance among Norwegian political leftists. It was no longer simply a matter of how to most effectively organise actions to combat porn and prostitution, but one of language and discourse analysis. From now on, it became increasingly "abusive" to speak of the prostitutes as "victims." As a consequence, almost any action was met with criticism over incorrect methods and an erroneous perspective on humanity. The leader of the Women's Front at the time attacked the Feminist Group Ottar and our actions against brothels in Oslo because we were demonstrating outside "people's working places." At this point, the Women's Front had become allied with PION. While feminists and neighbours stood outside the brothels and demonstrated, PION supported brothels as a way to get the prostitutes off the streets and into "orderly working conditions." After Sweden passed the Sex Purchase Act and thereby removed most of the street prostitution, PION's line of argument changed radically. Suddenly street prostitution was "safe and manageable," while the brothels were redefined as "underground" and out of reach of support services.

In the 1990s, PION and the Pro Centre gained influence. Despite playing different roles, their tactics were quite similar in that they managed to establish the premise that it is not possible to talk about prostitution without being directly involved in it or talking on behalf of those involved. This concept implies that one cannot discuss prostitution as a social phenomenon and that attitudes toward prostitution are guided by the number of individual prostitutes that can be pushed into the limelight. By making a few prostitutes "speak out," they control all knowledge about prostitution.

This manner of manipulating political views through emotion obviously demands that those who wish to dominate the debate have several examples to which they can refer. But happy and healthy prostitutes are not so common. Luckily, those who wish to "speak out" as happy prostitutes can claim anonymity, which means that they might appear with different names—giving the impression that they are much more numerous than they really are.

One might have believed that PION, as the self-designated mouthpiece for Norwegian prostitutes, had support from several prostitutes who could come forward and explain that they had chosen prostitution themselves. But in the 1990s it became clear that the recruitment among prostitutes was rather low, and PION continued to promote criminologists, lawyers, and social workers as their spokespersons.

However, when Sweden passed the law that criminalised the johns in 1999, "Gitte the Prostitute" suddenly appeared in the debate in order to offer a "feminist" argument against the ban on purchasing sex and for the legalisation of prostitution.

Since 2000, "Gitte the Prostitute" has been an active debater and lobbyist against the Sex Purchase Act in Norway, and it seems that since then certain arguments have entered the discourse: that prostitutes have more power than you might think; that in reality they are the ones who are abusing the johns; that nobody but the prostitutes themselves may talk about prostitution; that fighting prostitution is the same as fighting the prostitutes.

PION's line of argument gradually spread to the autonomous movement in Oslo, where activists had previously been engaged in the fight against brothels and strip clubs. For us they had been a great resource because many of these people were easy to mobilise and quick to attend demonstrations. Unfortunately, toward the end of the 1990s, the autonomous movement adopted liberal stances on prostitution. This was a major blow to our ability to mobilise at the grassroots level in Oslo.

Border Trade and New Alliances

The feminist movement was unable to resist this massive onslaught, and the porn and prostitution industry was allowed to establish permanent strip clubs and brothels disguised as massage parlours. At the same time, the cross-border trade between the northern Norwegian county of Finnmark and Russia became apparent in 1993–1994. A network made up of the Russian mafia and Norwegian criminals made sure that there was an explosive increase in the trade of women, which again led to major demonstrations and the mobilising of the local communities against prostitution. Self-proclaimed sex liberals and the prostitution lobby, especially in Oslo, accused the demonstrating activists in Finnmark for harassing lonely men and for being racist toward the poor Russian prostitutes. But the actions finally led to an opening up of the media, and we managed to have a public discussion that touched the heart of national politics.[44]

---

[44] See Marit Smuk Solbakk's chapter in this book for more information on these events.

In the wake of this new phase of prostitution history, new alliances emerged. The Northern Network Against Violence and Prostitution (Nettverk i Nord mot vold og prostitusjon) was created by feminist organisations from Norway, Finland, Sweden, and Russia. In the years that followed, Network North took part in many international conferences against prostitution and forged important political bonds. Contact with feminist activists from other countries provided the Norwegian activists with more knowledge and motivation to fight for a legal sex purchase ban.

One Step Backward and Two Steps Forward

In the mid-1990s, Norwegian authorities assembled a committee whose purpose was to recommend amendments to the penal code's chapter on sexual violations. In a proposal of 1997, the committee suggested the liberalisation of porn legislation and a lowering of the age of sexual consent. These proposals were justified by the changes in attitude among the population, as well as the increasing sexualisation in public arenas. The resistance to the proposal by the Sexual Violations Committee reinvigorated the old alliance between traditional popular movements and the radical feminists, this time manifesting as the "Spontaneous Action Against Hardcore Pornography" (Spontanaksjonen mot grovporno), which in a short time gathered more than 100,000 signatures against the liberalisation of the law on pornography. This had an effect on the politicians, and in 2000 Parliament rejected the proposal. But porn liberals in the Supreme Court exploited Parliament's deficient handiwork, and in December 2005 they unleashed the free flow of porn movies by acquitting the editor of a Norwegian porn magazine for having printed hard-core pornographic pictures. The weaker formulation of the porn clause in 2000 led to a situation that was fully exploited. Indeed, at the same time as the Supreme Court set hard-core porn on the loose, we also saw an enormous increase in the prostitution market, especially on the streets of the big cities. Adding to the already well-established trafficking in women from Eastern Europe, the Balkans, and Asia, the prostitution mafia began to import hundreds of Nigerian women for the street market.

The prostitution industry, especially in Oslo, expanded at a near-explosive pace. The fact that many of these women were from Africa made this traffic very visible. Men complained that they could no longer walk on the streets without being accosted by "aggressive prostitutes." Or, as the leader of the Pro Centre, Liv Jessen, expressed it in the Aftenoposten in 2006, "I hear that people are reacting to the Nigerian women selling sex on the capital's main avenue and that they are aggressive in their marketing. It is thus a problem of order and must be resolved through police regulations."[45] Rather than penalising the johns, the Pro Centre preferred to use the police against the foreign prostitutes who took the customers away from the Norwegian "girls."

No doubt an important reason why Parliament finally supported the Sex Purchase Act was the massive increase in Nigerian prostitutes on the capital's main avenue. Before this, many possible "solutions" had been suggested: public brothels in the suburbs, official red-light districts in the centre of Oslo, deportations of foreign prostitutes, or prohibition of buying sexual services only from trafficked women. However, it was simply not politically possible or desirable to support proposals that included regulation of prostitution for reasons of law and order.

The Feminist Group Ottar has spent a great deal of time and effort expanding our arena of action. By demonstrating in areas where prostitution is prevalent with the slogan "Ban the Buying of Sex Now!" we have refused to compromise or to be bullied into silence. By being controversial and confrontational, we have ensured that public opinion has steadily drifted into a negative view of prostitution. People have seen the development of the prostitution areas, they have heard our claims, and they have taken a stand for the abolition of prostitution. This has been an important factor in our eventual success in changing the law. Another reason is the broad coalition of popular organisations and the feminist anti-porn activists that, if we ignore the break in the Women's Front in 1991, has lasted for more than 30 years. Many of the proponents of a sex purchase ban, both in the feminist movement and in the various political parties, have been loyal to this coalition. These are the

---

[45] *Aftenposten*, June 28, 2006.

most important lessons from this chapter of the campaign in Norway. Both of these reasons have been instrumental in the fact that we were ultimately victorious. This might be easier to understand if we take a quick look at one of our neighbours.

Just like Norway, Finland saw a dramatic increase in the trade of prostitution after the fall of the Soviet Union. However, the debate in Finland had a different outcome than it did in Norway. During the 1990s, Finnish and Norwegian activists organised joint demonstrations against the campsite brothels in the north. In both countries, the discussions led to proposals for legislation following Sweden's lead in passing a legal sex purchase ban. But rather than penalising the purchase of sexual services, the Finns in 2007 passed a useless law that forbids only the buying of sex from trafficked and forced prostitutes. Unfortunately, Finland has lacked a militant feminist movement capable of defining the terms of a public debate. In addition, there has been no efficient coalition of popular organisations and feminist anti-porn activists. In our opinion, this is the main reason why Norway and Finland have ended up with very different solutions.

Victory!

Like other Nordic countries, Norway has been comparatively spared the trade of women for the last 100 years. Until the fall of the Soviet Union, prostitution was limited to a small urban group that was often linked to drug problems. This situation has been the stepping-off point for the politics of prostitution. In other words, this is the background for Norway's purely social-political approach, as opposed to a feminist approach that highlighted gendered power relations. The focus has been on the small, marginalised group that has served as the local "commercial inventory." The politics of prostitution has been a holdover from earlier times. However, what worked well enough the last time that international society took a stand on widespread sex trade more than 100 years ago is no longer sufficient. In those days, the campaign against poverty—that is, measures to prevent the recruitment of women to prostitution—served to limit the trade. But today, with an almost infinite supply of poor women who may quickly and effectively be transported around the globe, these measures are no longer enough.

The social-political approach did not work in the northern areas when the prostitution traffic exploded at the beginning of the 1990s. And it didn't work 10 years later, when the prostitution mafia started to import hundreds of Nigerian prostitutes to Norwegian cities. If the market is to decide, we will swiftly see a situation quite like the one we had in Finnmark during the 1990s and on the main avenues of Oslo during the 2000s—namely, a sex market whose unbridled expansion met with no resistance in the public arena. This is why we need to stake everything on a feminist, normative approach that concentrates on the market and focus on the largest group within prostitution: the johns.

For the Norwegian feminist movement, which has promoted the demand that johns be penalised since 1983 without any breakthrough in the public sphere, it is almost impossible to believe our success. Inspired by the Swedish law of 1999, the Norwegian feminist movement set out on a strenuous, long-term campaign with the awareness that we would meet with considerable resistance. From 2004, when the leader of the Pro Centre, Liv Jessen, was given Amnesty International Norway's human rights award for her "fearless work for the rights of prostitutes," until the summer of 2006, progress was slow. The political establishment and the media were at this time uninterested in any arguments rooted in feminist politics. Many politicians, both from the Socialist Left Party and from the Labour Party, campaigned against the legal sex purchase ban by participating in rallies and appearances with the earlier-mentioned "Gitte the Prostitute."

But it was to little avail. In 2005, LO, the Norwegian Confederation of Trade Unions, joined the campaign for a legal sex purchase ban. Since then it has become more difficult to dampen the influence of the feminist movement. When the dam finally broke, everything happened incredibly fast. On May 1, 2006, the first female leader of the Confederation of Trade Unions announced the organisation's new standpoint on criminalising the johns.

Soon after, one of the major national newspapers published a survey that showed that 60% of the inhabitants of Oslo supported the demand to criminalise the johns.[46] The Oslo Labour Party took into consideration what these numbers said about their own voters and decided to support a legal sex purchase ban. Certain of victory, the leader of Oslo Labour Party told the media that "we aim to have a penalising agenda passed in the National Congress in 2007."[47] Thus the stage was set for the spring of 2007, when the National Congresses of both the Socialist Left and the Labour Parties, with solid majorities, supported the demand to criminalise the johns.

While the discussions concerning the Sex Purchase Act in Norway have to a great degree been social-political rather than feminist, the Swedish argument for the same law has a far greater gender-political dimension. The law that criminalises the johns in Sweden came about through Kvinnofridslagen, a legislative package that was supposed to counteract violence against women and the oppression of women. The Swedish law of 1999 has inspired activists in several countries. After 1999, the prostitution lobby`s progress has been slowed in Europe, if not entirely stopped. And it has had a political effect far beyond Europe, too. Before the law was passed, most people thought that the legalisation of prostitution was unavoidable and that it was only a question of time before we had German and Dutch conditions in every country. The pro-prostitution lobby moved forward while we were moving backward—slowly, of course, but we were nonetheless in retreat. Since the Swedish law was passed, it is our side that has been strengthening and moving forward. With its law against the buying of sexual services, Sweden demonstrated that the development of the sex industry is in no way unavoidable, that society may indeed interfere and take control, and that prostitution is about how women are perceived and about the development of society. To put it simply, it is about gender equality.

---

[46] *Aftenposten*, May 18, 2006
[47] "Oslo AP vil ha forbud mot sexkjøp," nrk.no June 7, 2006.

"Things Are Not Always as They Seem": Rhetoric and Politics in the Norwegian Debate on Prostitution

Anne Kalvig

The phrase above was the title of a thick pamphlet published in 2003 by the Pro Centre, the national authority on prostitution and relief measures for prostitutes. The pamphlet was compiled and sponsored by an advertising agency, Cox Communication (*Cox Kommunikasjon a/s*) and served as a contribution to the debate about penalising the purchase of sexual services. In this chapter I will take a closer look at the rhetoric used in this pamphlet as well as in other publications for which the Pro Centre has been responsible. I will discuss the responses they have elicited from other participants in the prostitution debate and also take a look at particular actors such as Amnesty International in Norway and the government-run website *sexhandel.no*.[48] By investigating the perspectives, notions, and concepts used by the different participants in the debate, I hope to bring to light any political development that may or may have a bearing on this topic.

In 2003, I was the leader of the Feminist Women's Front in Stavanger, and it was in this capacity that I received the above-mentioned pamphlet, made up of more than 70 pages printed on thick paper. The pamphlet arrived in the mailbox together with a letter that explained the pamphlet's agenda: to counter the myths about prostitution so that people could base their opinions on factual evidence. The last page of the pamphlet read: "Many have a strong opinion about prostitution. We think that people

---

[48] In English, *handel* translates into "trade," so the website's name explicitly states what it is used for: the buying and selling of sex.

ought to—but based on realities, not on myths." I have since lost the pamphlet, but it may be downloaded from the website of the Pro Centre.[49] The website states that the pamphlet was published in 2005, but I received it in 2003, two years earlier. Taking note of this is more than quibbling, for there is reason to believe that the information that "the people in the pictures are not identical to the persons described" (p. 73 of the pamphlet) was added at a later date, in the 2005 version. When it was publicly distributed for the first time, the pamphlet was criticised both by the media and by the feminist movement for withholding the information that the people described in the pamphlet were fictional.

Apparently, for the designers of the pamphlet and the Pro Centre, one way of "de-mythologising the field of prostitution" was to trick readers into believing that prostitution for the prostitutes discussed in the pamphlet was chosen voluntarily, and that it was so very fine that they gladly allowed themselves be photographed as representatives of this "profession." In the letter that accompanied the pamphlet (a letter sent to only a few people), we were informed that the persons in the pictures were not actually the persons discussed in the pamphlet. In line with this perspective, we have on pages 4–5 "escort prostitute Anne (33)," who stands before the Royal Castle waving a Norwegian flag and dressed in a traditional national costume. The text about her reads as follows: "When someone asks me what my profession is, I lie, but inside I am thinking: 'If only you knew. I wonder if you would have liked me as much if you knew.'" The woman photographed and presented as "Anne (33)," as I have discovered, can easily be mistaken for Rikke Øen, one of the designers of the pamphlet. Rikke Øen and Christina Lind compiled the printed matter in cooperation with the Pro Centre and others. At the time the designers belonged to the advertising agency Cox, which sponsored the publication. Other sponsors included a foundation for designers "with a cause," spearheaded by the paper producer Sappi. In a printed publication called *Global Showcase* (2003) by "Sappi—ideas that matter," the company details the disbursement of its foundation's

---

[49] http://www.prosentret.no/ Pro Centre and Cox Kommunikasjon a/s (2005 [2003]): "Ting er ikke alltid slik det ser ut som."

profits for that year. Øen and Lind are also photographed and shown on page 71 of this publication, and Øen is quoted:

> "When mention is made of a prostitute, a negative 'hooker' image comes to mind," says Rikke Øen, designer of the campaign. "The public forgets that prostitutes are also parents, shoppers, voters and taxpayers. To this effect, the photographs that make up the campaign show regular looking people, men and women in their homes or on the streets going about very ordinary, everyday activities. The campaign also points out that prostitution is not a condition. Most of the time, it is a choice made by fully operative, conscious human beings. A broader understanding of prostitution will lead the public to realise that prostitutes shouldn't be condemned or pitied.[50]

Rikke Øen, a designer by profession and otherwise a completely unknown name for those of us who were engaged in the debate about prostitution in those days, was able to set much of the agenda at the time of the pamphlet's publication. As seen in the quotation above, it has been important for her to stress that prostitution is a choice—at least most of the time—made by "operative, conscious human beings." We read that the campaign, as Sappi has called the pamphlet, is directed toward the media and decision makers, who are presented as responsible for keeping the myth alive that prostitutes are drug addicts, thieves, and heavy criminals. The campaign also takes up the task of destroying the stereotypical idea that prostitutes are weak victims who lack the ability to control their own lives.

Many reacted strongly to this pamphlet, and not just to the photographs of make-believe prostitutes and make-believe customers. I was personally contacted by journalists who thought that the trivialising, even partly alluring presentation of prostitutes was worthy of criticism. On pages 46 and 47 it is written: "My girlfriend always makes good money—she has the hippest clothes, and when we go out, she buys. She has a few regular customers and tells me that I should try it. Completely unproblematic, she says." It is uncertain whether the beautiful, smiling, black woman on page 46 really is "Ann-Camilla (22) from Stavanger," a cashier with a money problem

---

[50] Sappi Limited (2003): "Global Showcase," p. 70, http://www.signals.ca/pdf/Sappi_IdeasThatMatter.pdf

who tells about her girlfriend the prostitute, or whether she is the "high-class prostitute" described in the statement. The message, however, is absolutely clear: prostitution is about beautiful youth, consumption, and an unproblematic way of making good money.

In addition to the vapid personal information about "Ann-Camilla" struggling with her finances, there is a statement of factual information: "the political line of thought behind the laws is that prostitution first and foremost is a social problem that we generally relate to with social efforts and measures to change the general attitude." This information suggests that the law is only about social efforts and attitude changes, and not about the legal change that penalises the demand for prostitution. The message seems to be: "Just watch out, you who struggle for penalising the sex buyers, because not only are women prostitutes happy, beautiful young people, they also have the law on their side—to the degree that there has to be a law, for you see here that it is completely unproblematic!" At least the legislation is the theme of the subsequent pages (48–55) in the pamphlet. Under the heading "The View of the Pro Centre" (as if everything in the pamphlet isn't basically modelled on the views of Jessen and her Centre), we read that it is too early to say anything about the experiences of The Netherlands, which had legalised prostitution. Nonetheless, it is completely safe to say that Sweden's strategy of criminalising the johns is worthy of criticism, based on "experiences from other countries," none of which is mentioned. The Netherlands legalised prostitution (through brothel businesses) in 2000, while Sweden, as we know, had passed a legal sex purchase ban the year before that.[51] In the paragraph "The View of the

---

[51] Professor of Medicine Berit Schei, who was one of three members of the Norwegian working group that was to report the results of legalising as opposed to penalising in the above-mentioned countries, had no problem recommending the Swedish model rather than the Dutch. However, she was the minority of the working group that otherwise consisted of two men, the legal professor Ulf Stridbeck, and the police inspector Olaf Kristiansen, and therefore dissented in the report—Stridbeck, Kristiansen and Schei (2004): "Buying Sex in Sweden and in Netherlands: Regulations and Experiences." http://www.regjeringen.no/nb/dep/jd/dok/rapporter_planer/rapporter/2004/sexkjop-i-sverige-og-nederland.html?id=278400

Pro Centre," which naturally also ends the discourse about legislation in the pamphlet, it is emphasised that only social measures are advisable when it comes to prostitution, and that penalising the purchase of sex will make contact with the "actors in prostitution" impossible.

Perhaps it is appropriate at this point to ask what the current mission of Jessen and the Pro Centre is, as well as what it was at the time that the pamphlet was published. Page 60 of the pamphlet states: "The Pro Centre is a centre of expertise about the topic of prostitution. We systemise knowledge, share information and give guidance to support service providers, the authorities and the public." The following pages in the pamphlet describe this work, as well as the Pro Centre's work as a relief measure for men and women with prostitution experience. For the relief work and neutral-sounding tasks such as systematising knowledge, sharing information, and giving guidance, the centre had a budget of about 9 million kroner offered by the government and by the Oslo City Council, in addition to gifts from private donors. The development and printing of the pamphlet were components of this budget. Since the pamphlet represents women in prostitution as smiling, proud, and active above all else, and the buyers as only seeking a bit of extra contact (such as "Karl (55), single, receiver of disability benefits," on pp. 8–9 of the pamphlet), it becomes clear that the "expertise" of the Pro Centre is politicised. This was also evident when Jessen decided that the act would work against women in prostitution and that the Pro Centre had already chosen their side in the debate, even before the Sex Purchase Act became law and before long-term studies and evaluation statements from Sweden became available. In 2004, moreover, Jessen referred to herself as a "political animal."[52] It has rarely been contested that the national centre of expertise on prostitution was—and is—led by an outspoken person who is on a collision course with the political majority that finances her enterprise. Most of Jessen's utterances and texts, as well as the website of the centre, hammer the point home to the reader that the right to choose a life in prostitution should be fully respected. It is sometimes not a long stretch to interpret "respect" as "admiration," something I shall return to later.

---

[52] Bergestuen (2004); see below.

Incidentally, it is worth mentioning that our national centre of expertise has failed to update its information to reflect the change in the law. On their website, under the tab "publications," again under "pamphlets," and yet again under "information pamphlets" (the only document localised under "pamphlets"), there is a folder, available in 10 different languages, that informs us that the buying and selling of sexual services is legal in Norway.[53] The page was last updated on June 17, 2009, so the error has persisted for some time. This speaks volumes about how unimportant this supposedly "neutral" institution of knowledge considers the political majority and the change in the law.

The use of language and perspectives in publications from and on the website of the Pro Centre obviously touches on many things—for example, whether prostitution is considered a conscious choice of profession with degrees of willingness, or as sexualised violence and an expression of the structural oppression of women. In the pamphlet "Things Are Not Always As They Seem," prostitution is generally referred to as the "purchase and sale of sexual services," as "sex trade that happens under marketing-like circumstances," and as "work." All the women who "came forward" in the pamphlet and who were later revealed to be fictional, were described as "working" as high-class prostitutes or street prostitutes. Presenting prostitution as work is not neutrally "systematising knowledge" and "passing on facts." Many would be strongly sceptical of this. (Other chapters in this book also discuss various examples of the politicised role of the support system for prostitutes.) In the next section, we will look at how another influential voice in the Norwegian debate, Amnesty International Norway, and its leader at the time, Petter Eide, embraced and rewarded Jessen and the Pro Centre's view of prostitution. We will also go on a little shopping spree at sexhandel.no before we examine some of the ideas about the Norwegian feminist movement's understanding of women as victims of prostitution.

---

[53] http://www.prosenteret.no/index.php?option=com_content&view=article&id=76:informasjonsbrosyre&catid=23:brosjyre&Itemid=60. Retrieved on February 24, 2010.

Amnesty Norway and Jessen as Allies

The designers Øen and Lind may be said to have had a certain amount of success with their "campaign," despite the criticism it also received, and despite the fact that the law criminalising the johns in prostitution was passed a few years after the publication of this thick, sponsored pamphlet. In any case, Amnesty Norway decided that their human rights award, to be presented for the first time in Norway in 2004, should go to Liv Jessen "for her untiring work for the rights of prostitutes for more than 20 years."[54] Many, such as the Socialist Youth League of Norway (*Sosialistisk Ungdom*, or SU), the Red Youth League of Norway (*Rød Ungdom*, or RU), the Red Electoral Alliance (*Rød Valgallianse*, or RV), the Feminist Group Ottar, the feminist Women's Front, and the Crisis Centre Secretariat protested the award. It was a biased contribution to the ongoing debate on prostitution, though Amnesty Norway at first tried to distance themselves from the criticism by claiming that they did not take a stand in relation to the political line of Jessen and the Pro Centre, but simply appreciated their "operative work." This was a logically impossible manoeuvre that Amnesty Norway did not repeat on later occasions.

A socialist newspaper, *The Class Struggle* (*Klassekampen*), printed my article entitled "Prize with a Bitter Taste: Is Not Prostitution Violence Against Women, Amnesty?" on October 10, 2004. In this article I claimed, among other things, the following:

> A national centre of expertise on prostitution has never been mandated with the purpose of strengthening prostitution. On the contrary, it is laid down in their given agenda to work to reduce prostitution. But how should one then interpret the fact that Liv Jessen is a Norwegian coordinator for Europap, an EU lobby that speaks of prostitution as "sex work" and which works for a change of legislation (i.e., legalisation)? What does it mean when Jessen repeatedly states that "the bad prostitution" is the kind that women are forced into through trafficking across the borders, whereas prostitution at home is about voluntary choices that women need to be respected

---

[54] Kaatee, Patricia (2004): "Jessen vant den første Amnestyprisen," http://www.amnesty.no/web.nsf/pages/77B60FE8CF632AE7C1256F0B0045F32B

for making? This completely contradicts what international documents have suggested, such as the Palermo Protocol that Norway has signed, which clearly states that "the agreement of the victim is without importance," because to exploit the weak position of a human being is a criminal action (about trafficking). It is worth remembering that equivalent expert and relief centres in other countries, such as Reden in Denmark, have chosen to unambiguously state that prostitution is violence against women, and that men need to be held responsible.... It is in this context that we, with wonder and great disappointment, experience that Amnesty embraces the line of the Pro Centre without criticism, even in the same year that Amnesty has launched its campaign against violence against women. For decades, the feminist movement has fought to establish an understanding of prostitution as violence against women, just like Sweden managed to with its legal sex purchase ban. What is Amnesty's view on prostitution and on violence against women?... When one reads the websites of Amnesty, one gets the clear impression that Amnesty supports Jessen and the political line of the Pro Centre, and not just her "operative work"; her attacks on and erroneous presentations of what the supporters of a ban actually want is left uncontested (we do not want to penalise prostitution, only the purchase of prostitutes), and a report about prostitutes who give thanks for Jessen's award has a presentation of their "joint campaign against penalising" that is not balanced by other opinions.[55]

Amnesty's spokeswoman, Patricia Kaatee, responded to the criticism in several stages, and she persisted in saying that no, prostitution is not violence against women,[56] and that there is an important difference between prostitution as a result of human trafficking and prostitution without a "similar system of backers," as she explained in an article

---

[55] http://www.kvinnefronten.no/Tema_politikk/Vold_mot_kvinner/171
[56] As clearly stated in the *Daily News* (Dagsnytt 18) on the same day as the award.

in *Klassekampen* on October 25, 2004.[57] Human trafficking is violence against human rights, even when the woman has given her permission to be traded across the borders, Kaatee further stated. Obviously, the Palermo Protocol of 2000 was thus harder to ignore than the UN convention of 1949, which states that prostitution is incompatible with the dignity and human integrity of the individual and harmful to the individual, the family, and society. Neither the Women's Convention of 1979 nor the Beijing Statement of 1995, which both state clearly that prostitution is violence against women, are given any weight in Kaatee's response. Since she is familiar with the Palermo Protocol's stipulation that the permission of the victim is not to be given weight, one might expect a consideration about the voluntary aspect of prostitution to be more complex. Instead, Kaatee says the following: "When prostitution cannot be regarded as anything but structural violence, prostituted women cannot be met with respect for the decision they actually make."[58] After that comes a peculiar barrage:

---

[57] Patricia Kaatee: "Prostitution: menneskerettighetene gjelder for alle," *Klassekampen*, October 25, 2004, http://amnesty.no/web.nsf/pages/AD15BF8711450A76C1256F38004 6E614

[58] In Kaatee's text on Amnesty Norway's website (see the previous note), she refers to my challenge of Amnesty on October 20, 2004, in *Klassekampen*. This is incorrect. I first had an article in *Klassekampen* on October 13, 2004, after that in *VG* on October 20, 2004, after that an additional article in *Klassekampen* on November 4, 2004, and finally one in the same paper on November 22, 2004. In the *VG* article, "The Failing Logics of Amnesty," I posed the following logical challenge to Amnesty/Jessen regarding the question about the difference between home-based and transnational prostitution, and the mantra of voluntariness: "Amnesty defends itself by saying that the opinions are so divided—and then supports the Pro Centre's illogical division of prostitution into a "good" and a "bad" form. This has awkward consequences: do the customers ask what choices the prostitute had when she became a prostitute? No, they are buying a commodity, legally. A prostitute in Poland, is she the victim of a "bad" form of prostitution when pimps are helping her to cross the Norwegian border? What changed—was she not in a vulnerable position in Poland, was her body not invaded by customers over there? The Palermo Protocol about the campaign against the trade of women and children clearly states that "the permission of the victim is without importance," when deciding whether a "trafficked" woman has been the victim of a criminal action. It is enough to have exploited her vulnerable position. But are men not doing this in homebound prostitution? To have trafficking, one needs a homebound market. When one cries out at home about choice and voluntariness, whose interest is one really promoting?" This was neither answered nor even considered.

> The Feminist Women's Front has defined prostitution as an im-
> portant structural cause of violence against women. An impor-
> tant argument is that equality in society may not be achieved as
> long as men buy, sell and exploit women. Amnesty cannot share
> this analysis. We do not regard prostitution as a cause of violence,
> but as a result of a gender based division of power and influence
> in a society that systematically discriminates against women.
> Prostitution is thus a problem along the same lines as other ex-
> pressions of discrimination against women in our society.

Now, it is not actually correct that we defined prostitution as "the
cause of" violence against women; we defined it *as* violence against
women. Such alterations of the opinions of the opponents may be seen
as part of the illegitimate, rhetorical tricks used during the heat of battle, or it may show that Kaatee has not actually understood our point at
all. There have been many more such awkward, tough, long-lived "mis-
understandings," as when Jessen claims that those who campaign to
criminalise the johns want to prohibit prostitution, not the purchase of
prostitutes, as mentioned above. It seems rather clear that Kaatee and
Amnesty Norway perform several verbal somersaults in order to keep a
safe distance from an understanding of prostitution as violence. Thus,
many people including myself feel that Amnesty Norway has become
a hindrance rather than a guardian when it comes to the state's implementation of human rights in legislation and in practice.

Sexhandel.no and Others Who Urge Tolerance for Prostitution
During the debate with Jessen, Amnesty and other participants who
fought against the understanding of prostitution as a manifestation of
men's violence against women, abolitionists could refer to the governmental Centre for Equality (*Likestillingssenteret*) as an ally. In the above-
mentioned debate, we referred to the paradox that Amnesty, as an organisation that pushes for states' implementation of human rights, spoke
against the Norwegian state in a reactionary manner. This was part of
their "defence" of human rights, because the governmental office that
worked for equality between men and women defined prostitution as a

component of violence against women. The Centre for Equality no longer exists (it closed in 2006), and the Commission of Equality and Anti-Discrimination (*Likestillings- og diskrimineringsombudet*) assumed the centre's concerns. In practice, this meant that the concept and the focus on "women" more or less disappeared and was replaced by "gender," in accordance with the development of academic feminism. Gender was then considered a "problem field" along with seven other foci, among them age, ethnicity, and sexual orientation. Of course, the Norwegian feminist movement protested the closing and the reorganisation of the earlier centre, but to no avail. The delegate (*ombudet*) of 2007, Beate Gangås, declared that she was opposed to penalising the purchase of sex. In the same year, the delegate warmly congratulated Jessen when she received the Award for Equality from the Confederation of Vocational Unions (*Yrkesorganisasjonenes Sentralforbund*, or YS).

But if feminism on the whole ceased to be an interesting and important issue in the public discourse, the situation was entirely different when it came to men.[59] The proof that it became politically correct to commit to men's issues while feminism gradually declined in governmental interest and expertise lies in the organisation "Reform—Resource Centre for Men" and their website.[60] As a politically independent foundation, though financed by the Ministry of Children and Equality,[61] this centre is supposed to be

---

[59] At the website of the Ministry of Children, Equality and Social Inclusion, equality is limited to a theme that covers "Integration of the Gender Perspective," "International Work for Equality," "Gender and Power," "Equality in the Working Space," and, finally, "Men and Equality." http://www.regjeringen.no/en/dep/bld/Topics/equality. html?id=1246. In February 2010 the temporary "Women's Panel" started its work by revitalising the debate about equality. The panel, which is a continuation of the earlier "Men's Panel" created by the Minister of Children and Equality at that time, Karita Bekkemellem, consists of 31 women from "different groups of society, vocations, ages, experiences and ethnicities," and they have, not surprisingly, chosen not to include any representative of the organised women's movement. (Ministry of Children, Equality and Social Inclusion, press release (2010): "Audun Lysbakken established the Women's Panel 2010 today." February 1, 2010: http://www.regjeringen.no/nb/dep/bld/presse-senter/pressemeldinger/2010/Kvinnepanelet.html?id=592578

[60] http://www.reform.no/

[61] This financing was not affected by the manoeuvring of the Parliament just before Christmas 2009, when the already minimal support given to run women's organisations was reduced by 30% without public debate.

oriented towards equality in its work and aid men practically in different phases of life and life situations with counsel, guidance and information, contribute to taking care of and developing diversity in men's lives, mobilise men's resources to development and activities in areas that have not been particularly prominent within the traditional male cultures, and otherwise contribute to the improvement of men's living conditions and life quality.[62]

One way of promoting diversity, development, and activities in men's lives was to establish and maintain the website sexhandel.no. This website was presented as a way to make men conscious about the connection between human trafficking and prostitution, in accordance with the Governmental plan of action against human trafficking of 2006–2009. However, the website, with its popular discussion forum, functioned above all as an information service for and among men who buy sex, where price and the quality of the "commodities" were discussed. Further, the "commercial" and "neutral" name of the website is not particularly well suited to increasing awareness about the violent character of prostitution. Instead it supports the understanding of prostitution as an exchange of services in a market between equal partners. A quick glance at the discussion forum shows that many of the men who speak out on the forum do not feel equal at all, but rather like victims of governmental feminism, money-greedy whores, and their own inability to access sex without having to pay for it. After the penalising act was passed by Parliament, the website continued as before, but the last contributions now seem to have been added during the summer of 2009. Special funding for the website ceased by 2010, but Reform has chosen to draw from their public resources in order to continue running it. It shouldn't need to be stated that the feminist movement has protested heavily against public money being used to run a service that shows solidarity with men's complaints and their internal exchange of sex-buying tips, but our protests have gone unheeded.

---

[62] http://reform.no/

On the home page of sexhandel.no, the Sex Purchase Act is noted, but with the webmaster's suggestion that the users continue discussing their issues (law violations) on the forum. The demand for a counselling service for johns is an issue that is marketed with a megaphone and is a signature function of both sexhandel.no and reform.no. Under various banners relating to the field of prostitution at sexhandel.no such as "Prostitution," "Female Prostitution," and "Clients," prostitution is defined as something that involves a buyer, a seller, and an exchange of money. There is nothing here about the damaging effect that prostitution has on women, or about the violent character of prostitution, or about the exercise of violence during the purchase of sex. Under "Prostitution in Norway," there is something about damages in the form of abuse within and outside of prostitution, which is apparently equal to the damage caused by the societal stigma about prostitutes. The banner "The Debate About Penalising" is introduced with the claim that "prostitution may have several harmful effects," and it is stated that those who campaign to criminalise the johns claim that a prohibition "exposes the fact that women are being exploited." The word "violence" first appears in the section arguing against penalties, and then in the guise of a claim that violence from pimps will increase.

The men who have been able to rattle on at sexhandel.no and representatives such as Jessen and Gangås all seem to agree that one of the biggest problems with prostitution—aside from human trafficking, which from their perspective is something quite different from prostitution—is society's lack of respect for the woman who prostitutes herself. The most prominent purveyors of this lack of respect, which apparently has horrendous consequences, are, of course, feminists of the radical kind. Toward the end of this chapter, I will take a closer look at this allegation about lack of respect and solidarity from the feminist movement, and at the use and definition of the word "victim" both within the women's movement and as used by Jessen and her allies.

Variants of Solidarity and Respect

Solidarity and respect can take many different forms. The same year that Amnesty gave the human rights prize to Jessen, there was much debate about being a feminist. Journalists and writers such as Hilde Charlotte Solheim (who is now on the board of directors at Reform), Helle Vaagland, and Hannah Helseth all went public and claimed that the demonstrations of the 8th of March, the International Women's Day, ought to cease, in an attempt to reform the way in which feminists organise. Representatives for the Feminist Women's Front and the Feminist Group Ottar, such as Marit Kvamme, Hanne Størseth, and myself, criticised their proposal for lacking a historical view and for being elitist and reactionary. The media-sector women mentioned above, together with Harriet Bjerrum Nielsen, the leader of the Centre for Women and Gender Studies (*Senter for kvinne- og kjønnsforskning*, or SKK)[63] at the University of Oslo at that time, encouraged young women not to become members of the Feminist Group Ottar or the feminist Women's Front because of our stand against porn and prostitution. Bjerrum Nielsen suggested instead membership in the Norwegian Association for Women's Rights (*Norsk Kvinnesaksforening*, or NKF), apparently unaware of that organisation's outspoken opposition to porn and prostitution and their poition in favour of a sex purchase ban.[64]

Our opposition to the idea that feminist organising ought rather to take place in the form of prattle between champagne and canapés in an apartment on the Westside (as suggested by Helseth during the above-mentioned debate), made Vaagland use her column space, titled "Feminist, Yes Of Course," in *Klassekampen* on March 22 the same year, to ask us to "go to hell." She continued by calling herself a "fashion feminist" and rambled on about how much she pitied herself, since she is "turned on by porn, even the bad porn." In some way, this admission to a taste for porn was meant to form the basis of a claim that there was now a roaring and much longed-for "feminist third wave" on its way. (Perhaps this wave culminated in the 2009 publication *Glitter*

---

[63] Now the Centre for Gender Research (STK)

[64] According to an interview with Siri Hangeland (NKF) in *Klassekampen*, March 17, 2004, and a report by Bjerrum Nielsen, Helseth, and Solheim in *Klassekampen*, 8th of March, 2004, "the feminist path onwards should not go through organisations such as the Women's Front or Ottar, who with their history and platform are against both porn and prostitution, and thus have very strong rules about the standpoint of their members."

Cunts—True Stories About Being Young Women.[65] Who knows?) She was not the only one to embrace porn in those days, and in 2006 an anthology about horny young women, *Pink Prose*, was published, with a chapter dedicated to defending porn entitled "Porn and Good Girls" by Heidi Sinding-Larsen.[66] Guest researcher Anne Sæbø from the Centre for Women and Gender Studies of the University of Oslo followed up on the trend and was lifted up on the wings of a variety of willing and lustful media when she spoke up for feminist prostitution in the shape of porn as women's liberation.

To illustrate how we regard the connection between porn and prostitution, and what empathy and solidarity is in this context, I quote here an excerpt from a longer article I wrote, published in *Klassekampen* on July 10, 2006. It is called "Feminist Prostitution," and it is a response to Sæbø's promotion and glorification of porn as liberating to women.

> Apparently, empathy and solidarity is a non-subject to academic/ journalistic defenders of porn. Repeatedly, what we are seeing is that women in well-paid positions, who work with text or with film, who seem to have discovered that sexuality and thus porn is something quite hardcore, and that there is an accordance between [sexuality and porn] that must have slipped the minds of the feminists of old. But few, if any, could imagine themselves being the ones to produce porn. That is the work of *other* girls and women, not of the office colleague next to you at the Centre for Women and Gender Studies, not your journalist colleague, but *someone* ought to do it. We assume that these women who ought to do this are women in a quite different economical, social and cultural position? Or is the goal something I think would concern the Actor's Association, that sexual portrayals are to become so "natural" and common to present on film, that where before one has really kissed, now one also

---

[65] *Glitterfitter. Helt sanne historier om å være ung kvinne.* Kagge Forlag (2009), Bonde, Tusvik, Sigrid and Gunnhild Magnussen
[66] Sinding-Larsen, Heidi: *Porno og pene piker*, in Roggen, Ida and Tonje Tornes (Eds.) (2006): *Rosa Prosa. Om jenter og kåthet.* Gyldendal Norsk Forlag, Oslo.

should really screw, so that the Theater Academy must include "this is how we screw in movies" on the curriculum? No, of course not; what was so glorious was the forbidden, so this should still be assigned to a particular movie genre, and made by particular people. But for ordinary, horny girls.

The level of reflection is depressing: In the prostitution campaigns, having to appeal to such infantile parameters as "would you like your daughter to be bought by other men," to confront men is ethically a low level of reflection. But we still do it, because tragically enough such kindergarten pedagogic is the only thing that might convince some men that women in prostitution are human beings with worth and rights, enough so that the UN reasons that women should be protected against prostitution. What then about the intellectual, academic feminists? They want an excuse they can use when they feel the urge to watch other women and men having sex for payment before the camera. For the women in porn are just exhibitionists. Just as women in prostitution are insatiable sex animals. For they are saying, are they not, something the testifiers of truth in media are milking for all it is worth, that they do this of their own volition, they decide for themselves! Has anyone wondered why women with porn and prostitution experience who experienced this as horrible (in retrospect, when they could allow themselves such thoughts) never expose themselves in the media? I know several of these, and they all say that the price would be too high, they are so damaged and broken that such exposure would shatter them completely—but the gods know that they would have liked to come forth with their testimonies of truth!

Liv Jessen systematically and actively ignores women who have come forth and told about their time in the porn and prostitution business. In her text *A Critical View on the Theory that Prostitution Is Violence Against Women*, these women are referred to as "the repenting sinners" and mentioned only in one sentence of a document of 15 pages, and not explored further.[67] Odile Poulsen and Louise Eek, from Denmark and Sweden respectively, have published several books on their experiences with prostitution in which they problematise the societal understanding of prostitution as a choice and convincingly provide firsthand reports on the violent character of prostitution and its role in the oppression of women and sexualised submission.[68] By coming forward, both Poulsen and Eek have paid a great personal price because, unlike women in prostitution who defend what they have experienced and/or are currently experiencing as personal, voluntary choices that must be respected, there is no cultural exaltation for women who describe prostitution as violence.

However, something Jessen and people who share her opinion are very concerned with, far more than and qualitatively differently from the women's movement, is the word and the concept of "victim." As I know from decades of activism, Jessen often lingers over the characterisations of victims, and sometimes one has an uncomfortable feeling about this lingering. "The whore image" is used as an example of how society should not think about women in prostitution (as broken, drug-addicted, repenting sinners, losers, shameful, fallen women), and as proof of the whore-madonna myth.[69] However, the persistent concern with "otherness" that should not be culturally reproduced is in fact repeatedly reproduced when one constantly talks about how "we" look at "them" that way. It begins to seem quite peculiar when Jessen herself constantly portrays women in prostitution as basically different, in a positive way: they are great, they have tremendous strength, they are glorious, they provide Jessen with a living, they have taught her a

---

[67] "Et kritisk blikk på teorien om at prostitusjon er vold mot kvinner" (2005) on the website of the Pro Centre. The text clearly bears evidence of being a translation of an English contribution to a conference, but this context is not mentioned on the website.
[68] Odile Poulsen: *Hustler. Min tid i prostitution* (Aschehoug, København, 2000); *Sirenesang. En fortælling om at overleve vanvid* (Aschehoud, København, 2006); the theater exhibition *Tvang—en psykologisk kærlighedsthriller* (2007). Louise Eek: *Spelat liv* (Bokförlaget Atlas, Stockholm 2002), *Att köpa eller köpas. Frihet og makt i sexindustrin* (Bokforlaget Atlas, Stockholm 2005).
[69] See, for example, "Introduction to 8th of March, 2004," p. 4. From the website http://prosenteret.no titled "Solidarity between women."

lot, they are heroines—"This is a gift I must give thanks for."[70] Thus, women prostitutes are not like other women, and the duality between prostituted and not-prostituted women is simply reversed; indeed, it is revitalised and supported. In Amnesty's panegyric interview with the human rights prize winner, Jessen is confronted with the "controversial" question about whether she herself could have been a prostitute ("Could Liv Have Been a Whore?"). The answer is, after some hesitation, that if she had been a foreigner and a single mother without means of making money and supporting herself (and the child, we assume), yes, then she could have sold sex in the Red Light District.[71]

Pardon? Is it not evident to everybody that all women, just for being women, might be prostituted? Whose interests do the good helpers protect when they turn this underlying message into a "naughty and stimulating" question about whether Liv could have been a whore?

For the feminist movement in Norway, this is not about women prostitutes' status as victims within a Victorian gender model; neither is it about their particularly heroic qualities. But from Jessen and other people's curious preoccupation with the idea of the broken, prostituted woman—the victim—another, less sympathetic impression seems to emerge. Perhaps a fascination with the culture of sexuality, so permeated with power relations, gives fuel to the not-prostituted defenders of prostitution?[72] Earlier we observed how Vaagland had similar problems understanding her own attraction to porn. Is this a stimulating field?

---

[70] The characteristics are drawn from the texts mentioned above and from the interview with Jessen by Amnesty Norway regarding the award, "Liv Jessen—Small, Big and Strong" by Svein Tore Bergestuen (2004), http://www.amnesty.no

[71] Bergstuen (2004).

[72] The same idea is expressed in the article "I Am Gina," by journalist Martin Gaarder (printed in *Samtiden*, March 2005), about a Nigerian woman, Gina, who is a prostitute in Oslo. The title is a parody of *I Am Dina*, a movie based on Herbjørg Wassmo's *Dinas bok* (Gyldendal Norsk Forlag, 1989), about the powerful, dangerous, and erotic Dina. Trine Rogg Korsvik of the Feminist Group Ottar composed a wonderful response to Gaarder's article in the newspaper *Ny Tid*, October 7, 2005, in which she questioned the "series of stimulating tales about the exciting life of people who really 'live strongly' by prosaic radical intellectuals who, strangely enough, let themselves be amazed that there are real human fates behind societal problems, and who have also forgotten that radical intellectuals traditionally have fought against prostitution," in a text that she titled "I Am Trine."

For us in the feminist movement, it is not; it is about all women's right to live lives without violence, about a societal change, and only to a small degree about sexuality as such. In a 8th of March speech from 2004, Jessen offers the following definition of respect:

> But what does it mean to give respect?... I will assert that only those who are in someone else's power may say if they feel that they are seen, heard or respected. This means that if the women in prostitution for example do not experience this respect, it is of little worth. Thus respect is not a word we can just use when we need it. We actually have to find out how it is received.[73]

Though it is not formulated in a crystal-clear manner by Jessen, this statement may essentially be interpreted as a view about respect being present only when those whom one is respecting agree that they feel respected. It is appropriate here to refer to an analogy from Tove Smaadahl of the Crisis Centre Secretariat, of which I have made use on various occasions, such as in my article "Amnesty—From Guard Dog to Break Pad":

> A close example to explain what this is about: when employees of a crisis centre experience how a woman for the eighth time returns to the husband who abuses her, does this mean that they ought to fully concentrate on women's right to choose a life of violence, rather than focusing on preventing men from being abusive, having men condemned for violence, and supporting women to break out of abusive relationships? Should we de-criminalise the abuse of women, seeing as some women choose to stay in abusive relationships?

In the battle over how to understand prostitution, the radical feminist movement has never claimed that women in prostitution are "only" victims without the ability to think independently or to make choices about their own situation. At every opportunity, we have emphasised that "victim" is a concept that expresses an imbalance of power between

---

[73] "Introduction to 8th of March, 2004" (p. 6), "Solidarity Among Women," http://www. prosenteret.no

people and is not a personal quality. However, the rhetoric of those who oppose the sex purchase ban uses a skewed definition. Our starting point has been the damaging effects of prostitution, individually and on a societal level, both in the short and long terms; that it is incompatible with human worth and dignity (as stated in the UN convention of 1949); and that criminalising the johns should be a strategic goal. Strangely enough, Jessen repeatedly claims that a focus on the john has been absent in the prostitution debate (see Jessen, 2005), a conspicuous and tactical move that serves to render invisible the fact that the feminist movement has focused continually on exactly this subject.

The rhetorical question we asked earlier—If there is no violence, then why should prostitution not be legalised and accommodated?—has rarely received any response. Jessen has, on a few occasions, gone quite far in promoting legalisation,[74] but the Pro Centre has publicly cautioned against Dutch conditions. For a long time, Norway toiled with legislation that contained the logically inconsistent prohibition against purchasing sex from persons below the age of 18, while the purchase of an 18-year-old body was legal (the sexual age of consent being 16, and there being no law against earning money before turning 18). Luckily, this is no longer the case. However, we owe no thanks to the Pro Centre for this, no thanks to the unorganised representatives of academic feminism, and none to the political elite. Despite their million-kroner budget, sponsored propaganda, political contacts in the higher circles of officialdom in Norway, and spokespersons in various media positions; despite their countless anthologies defending the trade of porn and prostitution and their tireless efforts to undermine feminist, radical, and collective campaigning and organising, the grassroots movement prevailed with its understanding of prostitution as something that affects everybody. In solidarity with all living and dead victims of the porn and prostitution business, we have now reached general agreement that the exploitation of human beings in this manner is not to be legal.

---

[74] Jessen (2005), p. 13: "They [the prostitutes] ought to have the same rights as other citizens and we ought to rid ourselves of facts that prevent this."

What about the trust put into a support services system that, for so many years, has gone on record as opposing a sex purchase ban and still seeks to present prostitution as something that has to do with heroism and strength? Outside of the network run by Jessen, a relief aid project for women who have left prostitution has now been established, based on the Reden model (the Danish equivalent of the Pro Centre that operates with the understanding of prostitution as violence), called "Nordic Swans." This network has been established through years of activism and, one hopes, is one of many emerging alternatives to existing support services that oppose the political majority.

Johns and Activists in the Sami Area

Marit Smuk Solbakk

This is a tale about what happened when prostitution made its entrance into to the little district called Tana in the county of Finnmark, in Northern Norway. When the border between Russia and Norway was opened in 1991, a cross-border trade swiftly developed, and we all went shopping and talking to people on either side of the border. Many of the Russians who came over to sell their merchandise spent their nights at the Skiippagurra campsite during the weekends. In the beginning there was some clash with the local merchants, but it soon dawned on people that the Russian trade attracted consumers. There was simply more trade as a result. During the first years after the borders opened, there was a lot of life during the day at Tana Bridge and at night at the Skiippagurra café. Then the rumours began to spread about drunken youths at the campsite.

In the daytime, the café seemed like a normal place, with the Russian trade and a lot of social interaction among the people. Then I heard the rumours about the drunken kids and started to wonder what happened in the evenings. I worked with a few women from Skiippagurra who told me what was going on at the campsite. What I reacted to most strongly at the time was that young junior high school boys were there drinking with adult men. My colleagues had also heard that there were many women and a lot of excitement in Skiippagurra. One day I received a phone call about organising a demonstration. The woman who called told me that there was now no longer any doubt that prostitution was occurring at the Skiippagurra campsite.

The Campaign Begins

In the late autumn of 1993, we mobilised 100 demonstrators to protest the sex trade around the Skiippagurra campsite. After this demonstration, it took us a long time to mobilise another big demonstration, even though the prostitution was expanding and we noticed that the attitudes around us were changing. We were uncertain about what we should and could do to stop the trade in women, and we simply lacked a plan. Adding to that, it was hard to mobilise because those who had participated in the first demonstration realised that they knew too many of the people who frequented the campsite. Soon another campsite was opened that also functioned as a brothel. It was located at the highest point of the Tana Valley, just by the border of Finland, and was called "Jungle Camping." Thus, we had two places where we had to campaign against the trade in women, and during the next few years we held several demonstrations against these brothels, even though only a hardcore group of six women was participating.

We were few, and the johns tried to frighten us from demonstrating. The small actions we organised were challenging and mortally dangerous. Johns tried to run us down, pointing their cars right at us and accelerating. The controversy received quite a bit of media attention both in Norway and in Finland, and we had support from people, but the situation was also heightened for us. The populace was divided in their view on the prostitution traffic. Many thought that we were the ones who gave Tana a bad reputation and that it was better to keep silent about what was going on.

In those days, many chose to believe that prostitution only involves those who choose to partake in the trade—in other words, the prostitutes, the johns, and the pimps. The pimps were those who made a profit out of the trade, whether it was as the owners of the campsite or those who directly sold the women to the men who bought them, or the ones who seemed more removed, such as taxi drivers and bus drivers, or the young boys who drove the johns around. The johns were often drunk, so the young boys got to drive nice cars and happily assisted in the transportation. Long before the district decided to act, many changes in the attitudes and patterns of the area had already taken place.

Prostitution as a Countryside Phenomenon

The prostitution traffic soon spread throughout the county of Finnmark. In Alta, the "River Camping" site was opened and run as a brothel. However, when local entrepreneurs tried to create a brothel near the campsite of Karasjok, we had already begun our demonstrations in Tana, so in that district the brothel was stopped before it could start.

Tana became the centre of the prostitution traffic. There were several reasons for this aside from its geography. Organised prostitution usually takes place in the city, where poor girls from the countryside are lured into the sex trade. In Finnmark, by contrast, there were prostitutes from the big city of Murmansk who travelled to small local communities. In the city, it is possible to avoid the prostitution by just staying away from the red light districts or simply closing your eyes. Even if there were many who tried to do this in our district as well, it was really not possible. The organised prostitution affected the whole of society, and it was impossible to pretend that we didn't know what was going on. The limits of acceptable contempt for women in society quickly deteriorated. In Nuorgam, a small village with only 50 inhabitants but a booming cross-border trade, the local café arranged topless serving. In Varangerbotn, a municipality of 800 inhabitants, a strip show for women and men was organised with many hundreds of onlookers from near and far. We attended such events to look the audience in the eyes, and we were not well received. Afterward, we were almost blamed for the problems that they later had with running the café in Nuorgam.

I have mentioned a few of our difficulties when it came to organising our resistance. The most difficult part was that everybody knew everybody. But that was also our strength. It was not the first time that the women of Tana organised a demonstration and marked their resistance against events in the district. During the mid-1980s, there was a widespread incest case in Tana, in which several of the most prominent men in the district were involved. When the issue became public, we held a demonstration to show our disgust for this environment in lower Tana. Many who participated in this demonstration came to play a central part in the resistance to the prostitution traffic in the area 10 years later. The environment of abuse in Tana was extensive, and several persons were convicted for sexual abuse against children. Even then, the attitudes were such that we who openly resisted incest and abuse were told to be considerate of the families of both the victims and the abusers.

This pervasive attitude was a problem when we tried to draw up a plan for closing the brothels. There were outspoken and unspoken demands concerning all the people we had to consider: the relatives, the families, the Russians who were married to men in the district, those who were sad and those who were sick. There were many to consider, and all of these special cases effectively demanded that we just keep silent about the whole thing. One part of Sami language and culture is to approach a topic indirectly, and in the beginning I adhered to this rule. However, it was not long before I started to speak frankly about things, at which point I was accused of having a "filthy mouth." The johns were partly protected by this requirement not to communicate problems directly. We who protested and confronted the problem were considered the rude ones—not those who, through their actions, influenced the development of prostitution in the area. This attitude communicated to me that the district really did not understand the seriousness of the situation.

This state of affairs continued, and everything could be bought cheaply: liquor, drugs, and women. There were brothels with all the licenses. In the spring of 1999, the graduates of Vadsø High School arranged for special status rewards for those graduates who bought a Russian prostitute. If there is anything we have learned in our district, it is that prostitution is a social problem that affects everybody. This is why the sex trade must be confronted on a social level, that is, politically, for the effects of prostitution are everywhere, and not just in restricted areas that can be avoided.

In the beginning the police were not present in the battle against this new type of crime that was spreading in our district. The pimps were treated as good citizens. If anyone was about to be arrested, it was ourselves and not the johns or the pimps. The district sheriff of Tana demanded paperwork and applications for permits to demonstrate. Police in other districts advised us that it was not necessary to have such permits; we had to deliver information about the time and the place of the demonstration, but not an application like the one he had demanded. When a new district sheriff was appointed, things improved.

The last violent demonstration took place in the summer of 1998. During this demonstration, a journalist from the newspaper *Nordlys* was physically attacked by Frank Sandberg, brothel host and owner of the Skiippagurra campsite. Despite this, Sandberg had the nerve to call the district sheriff to have the police remove demonstrators. The police arrived and asked us to leave, but there were many of us and we refused. From then on, the demonstrations were more peaceful.

The Campaign Spreads

We made contact with women activists in the south of the country in 1996. Asta Håland from the Feminist Group Ottar (*Kvinnegruppa Ottar*) called me after I had been featured in a newspaper article in which I had threatened to post a list with the names of all the johns at the local supermarket. Asta called to tell me that this could be dangerous and asked if I had a plan. I had not actually planned to put up the names, but the phone call led to further contact. We agreed to formulate a plan and create an organisation that was later known as the Northern Network Against Prostitution and Violence (*Nettverk i Nord mot prostitusjon og vold*).

Tana is a core area of Sami, and around one-third of the municipality speaks Sami. We Sami people had been particularly happy when the border to Russia was opened because we could finally come into contact with our Sami relatives on the other side. Through the Sami feminist organisation *Sáráhkká*,[75] we made contact with Russian and Sami women, also with the purpose of having the question of prostitution brought up by the Sami Parliament.

The zenith of the traffic in prostitution was reached during the years of 1997–1999. By then, the pimping mafia was well organised on both sides of the border. At the same time, we had organised. The Northern Network Against Prostitution and Violence was created in December 1997 as an alliance between *Sáráhkká*, the Feminist Group

---

[75] The organisation is named after a Sami goddess and protector of women.

Ottar, the Swedish women's shelter organisation *ROKS*,[76] the Crisis Line in Karasjok, and several Russian feminists who came over to Norway. Some also arrived from a Crisis Line in Murmansk. This was true cross-border cooperation. Since earlier days, we had a natural cooperation between activists in Norway and Finland, as we share both borders and problems. After a while, Russian organisations joined the Network, but sadly, because of the difficult economic situation in Russia, the activities of the Russian feminists were mostly limited to the area around Murmansk. Several Russian women living in Norway functioned as consultants. They insisted that we should not say "Russian prostitutes," just "prostitutes." It was difficult for Russian women and girls to live in Finnmark during this time, as they could hardly leave their homes without being harassed with offers from johns. The advice on how to use language with care was a good one that saved us many problems.

Now things were happening in a more organised manner all across the area. In 1998, the local council of Tana demanded a legal sex purchase ban in order to stop the increased trafficking. We arranged a large and successful conference in Tana toward the end of June 1998, and on November 25th of the same year, we organised a torchlight procession across the Sami Country Bridge between Norway and Finland, with several hundred participants. A youth group and a men's group were organised, both for the abolition of prostitution, and there was a lot of activity within the Network. Later on there was a rift between us and the activists in Finland because they were opposed to women-only organising. The youths wanted a group of their own, and we wanted the men to organise themselves. Among the men who were opposed to the prostitution trade in Tana, opinions were divided. Some wanted to penalise all the participants in the trade, while others agreed with us that responsibility lies with the johns. What seemed very clear was that the men had more need for discussion than the women. We had been discussing and had been active since 1993. In a busy situation, it was necessary for men and women to organise separately.

---

[76] ROKS—Riksorganisationen för kvinnojourer och tjejjourer i Sverige (the national organisation for women and girls' shelters in Sweden). ROKS aims at safeguarding the common interests of the shelters in their work against male violence against women.

Discussions and planning activities took place throughout the autumn of 1998. By the time 1999 rolled around, we had a plan to organise demonstrations outside of the brothels every Friday evening for six weeks. The campaign started with a 8th of March demonstration and a well-attended public meeting at Tana Bridge. This was a good test of how well we would be able to mobilise. Together with the local authorities, we arranged an information meeting for the district leaders about prostitution and our plan to abolish it. Tana consists of many small villages, and during the spring of 1999 we arranged meetings with all 33 village councils. This was not always a peaceful event, especially when we publicised our plan of action.

As mentioned earlier, there were two campsites in Tana at this time that functioned as brothels. One was the campsite in Skiippagurra run by Frank Sandberg, who was not from Tana but from Båtsfjord. The other campsite, "Jungle Camping," was in Laksnes, in Sirma near the border with Finland. This campsite was run by Reidar Varsi, a "son of the village," a status that made it more difficult to attack him. Our plan was to have demonstrations every Friday evening for six consecutive weeks from mid-March through April. However, we were uncertain about how many demonstrators could be mobilised on a Friday evening, and for this reason we decided to begin our first two demonstrations at the "Jungle Camping" site in Sirma so that we could also mobilise the Finnish activists. Strategically, this was a good choice. It would not be so difficult to mobilise people of Tana to demonstrate against the brothel in Skiippagurra, since the owner was not from Tana. To demonstrate against "Jungle Camping," which was run by a local, was a different matter altogether. Thus a difficult debate began, and many people, especially from Sirma, did not want to demonstrate.

The Campaign Becomes Critical

Rumours started to spread, including a very pervasive one that my husband Aage was a john, and that this was the reason I was engaged in the campaign for the abolition of prostitution. It was suggested that someone should put up a list at the local supermarket of all my lovers during my youth to demonstrate how loose I was. The municipal medical doctor,

Sigrun Winterfeldt, was reported from time to time to be getting a divorce. The fact that I actually had relatives who frequented the campsite brothels was used against me. I received many less-than-pleasant phone calls and finally had to get an unpublished phone number.

When the situation became critical, just before the weekly Friday demonstrations we had planned, we also encountered the problem that many of the politicians—both those in the local council and those of the Sami Parliament—were afraid of becoming personally associated with our campaign. This problem was, for the most part, solved when the President of the Sami Parliament, Ole Henrik Magga, appeared and made a speech at the first demonstration in Laksnes. This translated into an enormous advantage for us.

The young clergymen of Tana also turned out to be our allies. These vicars were rather active in the resistance against prostitution. They rallied the candidates for confirmation and other young people and, together with the older members of parishes, they turned out for the demonstrations in great numbers.

The health services personnel and the medical doctors were also key supporters. They brought with them the perspective of the social-medical consequences of the trade in women: increased violence within the families, alcohol damage, and a steady growth in sexually transmitted diseases. The doctors were under enormous pressure, since they were bound by the oath of confidentiality. The municipality's medical officer, Sigrun Winterfeldt, was attacked from all corners. The pressure on her was very strong, particularly because as the leader of the Health Council, she was the one who had closed the brothels in the first place. The police did nothing, because it was legal to buy women in those days. The brothels in Tana were thus closed with the aid of health and hygiene laws. Only later were the pimps actually prosecuted, but not all of them were convicted. The local council was generous to us and provided office space for the coordinator, who was hired by the Northern Network in 1998–1999.[77] We were also allowed unlimited use of the local council's copy machines.

---

[77] Jane Nordlund was hired as a coordinator from April to June 1998 in order to arrange a conference on prostitution. Asta Håland was subsequently hired from November 1998 to March 1999 in order to arrange demonstrations and take care of the presswork.

National Attention

Many central politicians visited our districts at this time. I wondered what the Minister of Justice, Mr. Dørum from the Liberal Party, was doing here, as I knew what his opinions were. We had held a couple of meetings with Dørum, who had been influenced by his years in the Church's City Mission and thus was very much opposed to criminalising the johns. When I look back at these things, I understand that he was there with a political agenda to quench the fire. At this point, the demonstrations in Tana had by and large set the agenda for the debate about prostitution across the entire country, and the journalists now called us before they called Dørum or the Pro Centre about the situation. Dørum was simply trying to regain the power to establish definitions. A prominent politician from the Labour Party, Rune Gerhardsen, also came to visit and expressed his opinion that it would be appropriate to also penalise the prostituted women.

One result of this "much ado" and all the visits from politicians was that a lot of money was coming to Tana—money that was earmarked for children and youth. The Skiippagurra Festival is one result of this. The first two times this festival was held, the municipality covered most of the expenses. Nowadays, when we finance it ourselves, we can say that the festival is a fruit of the activities connected to the campaign against the prostitution trade. The youths really took control and made a grand effort to change the situation in the district. While the battles raged most furiously, we arranged the Rock Against Prostitution, as well as concerts with Arja Saijonmaa and Kine Hellebust. The Skiippagurra Festival became a continuation of the campaign to abolish prostitution.

Skits, puns, and jokes have been a part of the battle for the majority opinion, something that still goes on. There have been many puns. "Gurra" may mean both "cleft" and "pussy." "Skiippa" means "boat," but may also be interpreted as "skihpa," which means "sick." If the intonation is put in a particular way, the place name Skiippagurra may in the Sami language mean "sick pussy." The ridiculing of Tana still goes on in many places. For example, the Norwegian female ski team, with Kristin Størma Steira from Tana in front, performed as Russian prostitutes from Skiippagurra at a press conference for the Norwegian Skiing Association a few years ago. I assume this was designed to ridicule those of us who are opposed to prostitution. Many people still refuse to acknowledge the consequences of prostitution in their society.

Victory Goes to the Women

The campaign against the brothels lasted for 10 years from start to finish. We staged the first major demonstration in 1993, and the pimp Frank Sandberg was finally convicted in 2002. Reidar Varsi was released. For many years I seemed to have two jobs, one that was paid and from which I made my living, and another that took up just as much time but which was unpaid. There were phone calls day and night, even at my workplace, especially during the year that I had a secret phone number. The press arrived from near and far—mostly from Norway and Finland, of course, but also from Germany and England. We travelled to conferences and held speeches in Sweden, Finland, Russia, Denmark, and the US. One of the things I remember best was that we were always photocopying. If we saw a copy machine, we photocopied flyers. We always had an original in our purses just in case we came across a copy machine.

There were threats and rumours—many rumours. Sometimes it felt as if we were surrounded by the enemy. But in addition to the massive attendance at the demonstrations by the people of Tana, we also received many nice letters from all over the country.

What do I think when I look back at these years? In retrospect, it was a very good time. It was pretty hard at times and very tiring, but it is absolutely fantastic that we finally succeeded. It was tough when people sighed when they heard my name, but more than anything else, I am proud of what we achieved in our district. I am certain that there would not have been a law against buying sex in Norway if we, here in Tana, had not taken the blows.

"Radical Feminists" and the Dispute About How to Understand Prostitution

Tove Smaadahl

For more than 100 years, the feminist movement has campaigned for women's rights and equality between men and women. The struggle has been tough. We have met with a lot of resistance, but it has produced great results. We have achieved many important economical, juridical, and, not least of all, social changes.

Women Organise in the Campaign Against Men's Violence Against Women

In Norway, the Crisis Centre Movement (or Shelter Movement) emerged from the new feminist movement. During the 1970s, many women engaged in the campaign against sexual oppression. Many had come together from the old and new organisations and cooperated in taking action. Despite differing political views and experience, women had a common interest in this cooperation and agreed to display solidarity with women exposed to violence. The Camilla Shelter was established in Oslo in 1978, and by 1985, 29 crisis centres and crisis lines were established around the country. Eventually there were 51 women's shelters, and the number has been stable to this day.

To begin with, a lot of time went into trying to obtain funding for running the shelters, and one also had to deal with debates about paid or voluntary work, a feminist approach or otherwise, and forms of organisation. Despite this, the Crisis Centre Movement managed to coalesce around a common ideological platform in 1982. Men's violence against women needed to be confronted both on an individual and a societal level, and it was understood to be a result of unequal power relations between women and men. The platform read:

> VIOLENCE AND ABUSE AGAINST WOMEN IS A PART OF THE OPPRESSION OF WOMEN. THE OPPRESSION OF WOMEN IS A SOCIETAL MATTER.
>
> Thereby, we wish to address any aspect of society that legitimises, supports and maintains violence against women. In this work we are party-politically neutral, and not connected to any particular organisation or religious denomination.
>
> WOMEN UNITE IN THE CAMPAIGN AGAINST THE OPPRESSION OF WOMEN—PRIVATELY AS WELL AS PUBLICLY.
>
> In addition to the running of the various crisis centres and phone lines, we want to influence society in changing its views on violence against women.[78]

The ideological platform that problematises men's violence against women as a phenomenon of its own has been a great advantage in our work as political agitators. It has made our mission clearer and provided a common message all around the country. The Crisis Centre Movement's National Conferences have been important arenas for debating and developing politics, in which political standpoints were stated in the form of decrees.

In 1994, 22 crisis centres formed the Secretariat of Crisis Centres. Prior to this, four shelters had left the Crisis Centre Movement and established the Norwegian Society of Women's Shelters in 1990.[79] The Secretariat of Crisis Centres, which continued its work based on the original platform, had as its objective to strengthen the shelters' external activities by uniting as many of the existing shelters as possible.

---

[78] Extract from the platform of the National Conference of Crisis Centres in Tromsø, 1982.

[79] There was unrest in the Crisis Centre Movement because shelters that had not agreed to the platform were to participate in the annual National Conference. After a while, these shelters chose to stay away from the National conference, and in 1990 they formed their own crisis centre organisation, The Norwegian Society of Women's Shelters [Norsk Krisesenterforbund]. See Jonassen, Wenche, and Kari Stefansen (2003): *Ideologi eller profesjonstenkning? En statusrapport om krisesentrene.* Høgskolen i Oslo.

As a political actor, the Secretariat of Crisis Centres has moved from being met with scepticism and suspicion to being regarded as an important deliverer of knowledge and political statements. The reasons for this are several: we have a strong media profile, we have participated in several committees and professional networks, and we have cooperated with scientists in the field. Additionally, we have offered opinions about various plans of action and published several reports and instructive pamphlets that consider the experiences of the crisis centres as a starting point.

The activity of the secretariat has also included several direct requests to the public authorities, as well as widespread lobbying. We are used as a consultative body for legislative proposals and other public accounts. The sum of all this has probably contributed to increasing our credibility as an "expert" on the problem of men's violence against women.

One of the most important takeaways from the 30-year history of the Crisis Centre Movement's campaign against violence and oppression of women is that the challenges must be approached from many angles and through different means. To create coalitions of different actors with the same objectives has been important in achieving results.

The Crisis Centre Movement Engages in the Debate About the Purchase of Sexual Services

During the 1980s, women's shelters had rules about not taking in women in prostitution. On the other hand, they supported the relief measures offered by others, such as the Pro Centre and Nadheim.[80] At the National Conference of 1982, the Crisis Centre Movement called for measures against prostitution but at that time did not place men who purchase sexual services on the agenda.

The debate about criminalising the johns was raised for the first time at the National Conference for Women's Shelters in 1998. The Bergen Women's Shelter then proposed the following resolution:

---

[80] Nadheim is a centre for women in prostitution in Oslo.

By penalising the clients we will limit the demand, and in this way limit the recruitment to prostitution and to the clientele. All of the experience that the Crisis Centre Movement has regarding women who are exposed to abuse of this kind justifies that the johns ought to receive penalties for their abuse of women. The slave trade of our time must finally come to an end.

This message was repeated in the form of a resolution in 1999 and again in 2002, in which the movement demanded that Norwegian politicians take responsibility for helping women out of prostitution by penalising the purchase of sexual services. Not everybody agreed that penalising was the right path of action, but the resolution gained a majority. The vision and the objective of the feminist Crisis Centre Movement is a society in which men and women are equal, and in which no one is exposed to discrimination, violence, or sexual abuse. In the internal debate, there was general agreement that prostitution is not first and foremost about poor women and social problems, but about a society where the lack of equality has contributed to the abuse of women in vulnerable life situations. Comparably, the effect of penalising men's violence in intimate relations is that women who are exposed to violence today have a claim to protection and the opportunity to improve their life conditions.

Important perspectives in the debate also came from the experiences that the crisis centres had with preventive measures, which illustrated that it is easier to change actions and attitudes in society if such efforts are supported by legislation rather than by purely social efforts that lack such legislative backing. It has been important not to underestimate the normative effect of laws.

Therefore, we never feared that the penalisation of the purchase of sexual services should provide a false sense of security for our own consciences, as many opponents of the ban thought it would. It is not about this. It is about using the law to give women in prostitution rights, protection, and relief measures that cannot be ignored or explained away. It is about placing responsibility with the men who maintain the sex trade, thus reducing the demand. It is about how punishment, as a pedagogical measure, will serve to discourage and change habits. Using this legislation will, in the long run, serve to equalise the living conditions and power relations between men and women.

Already in 2003, a crisis centre received a request to offer protection to a woman who had been exposed to trafficking and abused in prostitution. In the same period, the police gave notice that there were no safe havens for women who had been identified as victims of trafficking.

Our experiences, combined with the dearth of alternatives to women in prostitution, caused the Secretariat of Crisis Centres to apply for funding to establish a project that had the goal of combining physical security with relief measures for the victims. The RRSA[81] project was established in 2005 with financial support from the Ministry of Justice and the Ministry of Foreign Affairs.[82]

Since the Crisis Centre Movement had already defined prostitution as men's violence against women, there was little internal debate about whether the centres should take care of women exposed to human trafficking and who were abused in prostitution. What some feared was that a lack of knowledge about the needs of the women could lead to frustration among the employees of the shelters. But by 2006, after six months of running the RSSA, we had already evaluated the support given to the women. The title of the evaluation was "They Make Me Feel as if I Belong Among People," and it refers to a woman's words about how she had regained basic faith in herself as a human being. A better testament could hardly have been given to the workers at shelters. The experiences gained through the evaluation with the women who used RRSA also resulted in more credibility for the Secretariat of Crisis Centres in the debate about penalisation.

---

[81] RRSA: Re-establishing, Residences, Security and Assistance [In Norwegian: ROSA— Reetablering, Oppholdssteder, Sikkerhet og Assistanse].

[82] The RSSA project was established on January 1, 2005, after an application from the Secretariat of Crisis Centres in Norway. The mandate is to coordinate secure residences with access to necessary support and information to women who have been exposed to human trafficking according to the Council of Europe Convention, Article 4.

Network Against Prostitution and Trafficking in Women

In 2000, when Parliament passed the revision of the sexual legislation, they decided that the question of penalising the purchase of sexual services should be taken up again after two years, when one expected to have the experiences of the Swedish Sex Purchase Act on which to base the discourse. This did not happen, but the debate about prostitution did recommence, triggered by the focus on international prostitution and trafficking in women.

Against this background, the Network Against Prostitution and Trafficking in Women was established in 2002. The agenda was to make more progress in the campaign for the abolition of prostitution and human trafficking, not simply to focus on harm-reduction measures. In addition, the members thought that it was high time to direct the spotlight onto the most numerous group in the sex trade—the johns.

The earlier Centre of Equality, the Feminist Women's Front, JURK (Legislative Counselling for Women), the FOKUS-Secretariat (Forum for Women and Equality Issues), and the Secretariat of Crisis Centres established this network together, following a Nordic-Baltic campaign against trafficking in women and children in 2002. The Feminist Group Ottar, the Norwegian Association for Women's Rights, the district of Tana, Reden in Copenhagen and Stígamót in Iceland,[83] as well as individuals who had experience with prostitution and human trafficking, all joined the Network one after the other.

The Network promoted a unified view that prostitution is violence against women, and that prostitution and human trafficking are the result of inequality in society, where women are not economically independent. At the same time, we promoted the view of the UN Palermo Protocol of 2000 (signed and later ratified by Norway), where women's agreement to prostitution and human trafficking across national borders is considered irrelevant. We also promoted the protocol's mandate for support and juridical assistance to victims—that is, the women and children who are victims of prostitution and human trafficking.

---

[83] *Reden* is a Danish centre of residence and counselling that was opened in 1983 for women in prostitution, including those who are addicted to drugs. *Stígamót* is an Icelandic centre for counselling and information about sexual violence.

The Network organised a series of meetings and conferences to discuss the trafficking and prostitution of women and published a pamphlet detailing arguments for criminalising the johns in 2003, with Marit Kvamme of the Feminist Women's Front as a key contributor. The pamphlet was distributed to women, professional organisations, political parties, and others. It was also translated into English and published on the websites of the participants in the Network.

The publication of the pamphlet, which argued for penalising the purchase of sex and discussed the consequences for women in prostitution, was an important step in the campaign for the abolition of prostitution and human trafficking, as well as the campaign for invalidating the myths and attitudes of society.

Those who opposed the opinions of the Network quickly stepped into the public arena, and the level of debate was very intense during the period 2005–2007. Many lectures and meetings took place, and many newspaper articles and chronicles were written. Many in the Network took part in debates on radio and TV. The temperature of the debate was high until the Norwegian Labour Party decided to penalise the purchase of sexual services in its National Party Conference in April 2007. At that time there was a political majority in Parliament that supported a sex purchase ban, consisting of the Labour, Socialist Left, Centre, and Christian Democratic parties of Norway. The penalising Sex Purchase Act was passed in Parliament on November 20, 2008.

Is the Feminist Women's Movement Oppressing Women in Prostitution?

The definition of prostitution as violence against women implies the potential for action and, thereby, change. In the debate about women in prostitution, there are different views on whether women are victims or willing subjects who choose to prostitute themselves. The victim concept has different interpretations and is often conditioned by the understanding of "victim." When we talk about women as exposed to violence, it is because they are not acting subjects in their own lives. The crisis centres have always been concerned with the importance of supporting the individual woman in finding and experiencing dignity and strength in her own life, obviously in close connection with the need to change the external conditions that erect obstacles to her in this respect, or the "help to self-help" perspective. To live for a long time with a violent man, or in prostitution, have great consequences for women. It may be difficult to see the structural gender and power perspective. It is of crucial importance that the women themselves are active in the process of breaking out of an abusive and oppressive relationship, and at the same time understand what it is that they have been exposed to.

We in the feminist women's movement have been called many things, and it has been especially popular to refer to us as "radical feminists." Those who were against criminalising the johns claimed that "the radical feminists" had a definition of prostitution that in itself was oppressive. The critics further claimed that our ideology, understanding, analysis, and agenda fundamentally broke with the understanding that prostitutes themselves have about prostitution. We were criticised for not wishing to let the women in prostitution partake in the debate themselves.

The claim that the women were not allowed to express themselves is not correct. Throughout the years, with the ROSA project, among other things, I have met many of the women who have wished to break out of what they had been trapped in. Even if the women have not taken part in the public debate, this does not mean that we do not hear them. We have brought their stories and experiences to light in many different forums and debates. The reason why they have not wished to come forth has to do with the fact that these women have good reason to fear persecution directed both at themselves and their families. Furthermore, they tell about situations no one wants to experience, and that they feel shameful about. Our experience is that it is our strongest critics, whose understanding of prostitution as a choice with degrees of free will, break fundamentally with the reality that women in prostitution describe.

The women tell about serious physical, sexual, and psychological violations. They tell about force, threats, and pain. They say that they want out of prostitution, that they want another life. The ROSA project has managed to guide women out of prostitution and into a different life, and the women themselves confirm our belief that this works. Despite exposure to tremendous violations, these women have managed to find ways of surviving and maintaining the hope that there is a path out of human trafficking and prostitution. It is a difficult path. The women tell us that despite the experiences and the insecurities they still live with, many have begun to dare to hope for happiness and a better future. They tell us that they dare to feel the relief and the joy of being free from johns and others who had authority over their lives.[84]

Many claim that we "radical feminists" are labelling prostitutes as victims, and that we consider the men who buy sexual services to be abusers. This is how they describe the understanding of the gender-power perspective of the "radical feminists." We do wish to understand prostitution and other forms of abuse against women from this perspective, and we think that having an understanding of gender, power, and powerlessness is important in the campaign against the sexual violence that women in prostitution experience.

The unwillingness to discuss this imbalance of power between genders creates a need for alternative explanations for men's purchase of sexual services and other forms of abuse. Instead, the gender and power perspective is explained in connection with deviations from the norm. This transfers the focus on men's purchase of women's bodies onto "the others" instead—that is, "the ugly men," "the rejected men," "the men who have strong sexual urges," and so on. In this way, the image of Norway as an ideal country that enjoys gender equality is perpetuated. The Swedish evaluation "Punches in the Air" from 2004 shows that the consequence of moving the focus away from gender equality does not contribute to the prevention of men's violence against women and children. The upshot is instead that the man is *not* made responsible for his actions as violence. By understanding violence within a structure in which gender is connected to power, one may see how different arenas, actors, relationships, and types of violence are all connected.

---

[84] See the website of the ROSA project: http://portretter.no

Myths and the Lack of Knowledge Regarding the Consequences for Women in Prostitution

While carrying out an assignment from the Nordic Institute for Women and Gender Research in the spring of 2007, the Humanist Project team at the University of Oslo conducted a study about "Prostitution in Norway—The Opinions of Specialist Environments."[85] The report is based on interviews with 20 persons within the special field. Scientists, representatives from ministries and directorates, organisations, as well as a representative from Oslo Municipality, took part in the study. The report shows that even though there was general agreement in the special fields that the level of free choice varies and has many nuances, most of those interviewed were of the opinion that prostitution for the most part is about involuntariness and near involuntariness, and that everything from force to the lack of alternative opportunities gives the women in prostitution a bad starting point. It is strange, then, that Liv Jessen, the leader of the Pro Centre, among others, has clearly expressed that "we have to trust that the women can make their own choices, and that they choose prostitution." Or is it as the report shows that there are different opinions about prostitutes as acting subjects or victims even within the Pro Centre, and Jessen's particular view and definition of voluntariness is legitimised by her experience working in the field?

Liv Jessen has played a very central role in the debate about prostitution, taking a clear position against criminalising the johns. In view of her background as a leader both at a municipal support centre for women in prostitution and a national centre of expertise, one may question whether she has contributed to the maintenance of the myth that women "voluntarily" choose to prostitute themselves. What we can determine for sure is that these myths are, sadly, still thriving, especially among men who buy sex. The myths about women in prostitution often build on ignorance and preconceptions, and not on any gathered scientific documentation. For example, Jan Hansen, a john, in a contribution to the newspaper *Dagbladet* on April 23, 2007, wrote:

---

[85] "Prostitusjon i Norge—oppfatninger i fagmiljøene" (Humanistisk prosjektsemester, NIKKS).

Is it right that we should be regarded as criminals just because we sometimes seek to achieve health-improving intimate contact and normal sex? The prostitutes make a considerable contribution to the general health condition of many people.

In the contribution, Hansen says that he has 17 years of experience with buying sex in Scandinavia, and that the intimate contact received by *rejected* people adds to their everyday level of energy and well being. Thanks to the opportunity to buy sex, they can handle work and everyday life better. In a contribution to the forum on the website of Reform—Resource Centre for Men (http://sexhandel.no), we read:

What is this stupid expression that repeats itself all the time.... One does not buy a human being, one buys an hour of intimate physical contact and happy company because this is necessary. A conceptual understanding that lies far above the head of Marit Nybakk, I will be so rude as to claim.[86]

Both quotations show that the men legitimise and glorify the purchase of another human being and even claim membership in a vulnerable group as an excuse for abusing women.

In an article in the newspaper *Bergens Tidende* of April 20, 2008, an anonymous man tells about buying sex as a hobby: "It is like a kind of hobby. Some spend money on boats and cottages. I spend money on this." During the celebration of his own birthday, he ordered 22 women but bought only six, most of them from Eastern Europe: "I prefer them young and pretty, and the ones I buy are often very intelligent women with high education," he adds. He explains that he is fully aware that most of the women have men behind them, especially the women from Eastern Europe. During the interview, he admits that he also buys women from Thailand, who are often from poor backgrounds: "I, as a person, mean nothing in this market. If I do not say yes, someone else does. Shall I act as a holy...cow, and say no to a beauty who wants to sell herself?"

---

[86] Marit Nybakk is a member of Parliament representing the Norwegian Labour Party, and has been an active force in making her party support the sex purchase ban.

Many of the opponents of penalisation think that men do not buy women, but sex. However, the following comment illustrates that many men regard women in prostitution as a commodity, so they consciously buy from the "top shelves": "Once we ordered a lady.... She was fat. She could have been a trafficking victim! She ended up receiving payment just for showing up."[87]

Several studies show that men who purchase sexual services demand that the women in prostitution be attractive, bright, nice, warm, intimate, and professional, that is, generally of good calibre. They prefer a woman they can take on a hike with or go skiing with. Thus, the argument that they are only buying sex fails, since the demands on the women are great regarding "quality and content."

In Elin Kippe's report "Do Real Men Buy Sex?" (2004),[88] her profile of 20 johns shows that they defend their purchasing of sex with similar arguments: that prostitution is the world's oldest profession, a necessity of society; that men have strong sexual urges that must be satisfied or they could, in the worst case, abuse a woman; and that sex is a right for men and a duty for women.

What most of them cannot imagine is being a prostitute's boyfriend, according to Kippe's report. They do not want a woman who has sex with so many men. The prostitute is the sexually available woman with whom they can experiment with acts they do not want to engage in with their girlfriends or life partners. This coincides with the experiences related by women in prostitution. In the report "Relief Work for Victims of Human Trafficking—A Challenge" by Rachel Eapen Paul and Lene Nilsen (2009),[89] Vera states: "You feel used—like a thing. They pay for your body. You are paid for them using your body as they like. No one is interested in you as a person."

---

[87] From *"En analyse av unge menns forhold til sex-kjøp, gjennomført av Sosioraster Ltd"*[*An analysis of young men's attitude to buying sex, Research by Sosioraster Ltd*]. Dag Inge Fjeld and Karl Fredrik Tangen, December 2005–April 2006.
[88] *"Kjøper ekte mannfolk sex?"*
[89] *"Hjelpearbeidet til ofre for menneskehandel—en utfordring."*

In the same report, Nadia says: "I was visited by maybe four, five, six, ten men every day. It ruins your body." It is a widespread misconception among men who buy sex that the women in prostitution do not suffer, for they have themselves chosen this life. The words of Nadia and Vera disprove this. The men's mistaken notion also does not coincide with studies of the health problems and physical damage of women in prostitution. Research shows that women in prostitution universally suffer serious depression, anxiety, sleep disturbance, trauma, and suicidal thoughts, or actually commit suicide. Between 65% and 90% of the women experienced abuse or insufficient parental care in childhood; more than 60% of the women in prostitution suffer from post-traumatic stress syndrome, just like victims of torture and war; more than 80% experience serious and repeated violence from johns and pimps.[90]

To be in prostitution implies being exposed to a great risk of rape, battering, loss of freedom, sexually transmitted diseases, damage to skeleton, sexual organs and anus, unwanted pregnancies, and other physical and psychological damage. It is therefore important to ask: Why is it always the men's need for intimacy and satisfaction that should be met? Among the men who buy sex, is there a lack of knowledge about the consequences for women in prostitution, or is it just not relevant to them? And who is to do the "job" if most agree that they do not wish their daughter, mother, sister, or girlfriend to do it?

In Liv Jessen's book *The Ideal Victim* (2007), Per Kristian Dotterud, earlier leader of Reform—Resource Centre for Men, writes about how he experiences the Norwegian debate about prostitution: "The face of power in this discussion is primarily represented by the 'radical feminists.'"[91] He adds that the "radical feminists" have had a great impact. His definition of "radical feminists" includes the Feminist Women's Front, the Feminist Group Ottar, the Crisis Centre Secretariat, and the Secretariat of FOKUS. The other members of the network are,

---

[90] Marit Kvamme (2003): "Prostitusjon og handel med kvinner" [Prostitution and Trade in Women] Debate pamphlet. Network Against Prostitution and Trafficking in Women.
[91] Liv Jessen (Ed.) (2007): *"Det ideelle offer—andre tekster om prostitusjon."* Koloritt forlag.

oddly enough, not mentioned. In his article, he spouts an analysis of us and writes many things that are simply not correct, such as the claim that our reason for agitating for the abolition of prostitution is *not* to protect and help the women out of prostitution, but that the female role model that the prostitutes represent is morally challenging to us. Our opponents in the debate about a sex purchase ban often supported this view.

A woman is a woman is a woman. Whether she has been raped, battered by her life partner, or has experienced prostitution, she has a right to dignity, respect, and reparations. The agenda of the feminist women's movement has been for many years to establish support measures to help women escape debasing relationships, as well as to campaign against the structures that maintain men's violence against women. But no one can say that this has been a battle lacking spirited opposition. The greatest "opponent" today is perhaps the idea of an equalised society; this hides men's violence against women behind gender-neutral terms such as "partner violence," "family tragedies," and the idea that women volunteer for prostitution. I actually dare to claim that it is thanks to feminism and the courage of feminists, and not least of all their convictions, that we have support measures and juridical rights. At the same time, we need to acknowledge that some of the cases we have brought to the public agenda have not been easy to listen to, and for that reason we meet with resistance. We face opposition not only for ideological reasons, but also because facing the reality we are describing is so terrible for a democratic and so-called equalised society.

Despite all the criticism that we "radical feminists" have received, especially in our campaign for the abolition of prostitution and human trafficking, we are proud of the fact that our analysis and line of argument have had an impact. This shows that the work laid down by the feminist women's movement has not been in vain. And so we received with joy the new law that bans the purchase of sexual services in Norway and abroad. By passing this act, society signalled that there is agreement about prostitution as sexual violence and chose to place the responsibility for this violence with the abuser.

The Campaign Within a Governmental Party

Kirsti Bergstø

The Socialist Left Party of Norway (*Sosialistisk Venstreparti*, or SV) is a feminist and socialist party working for a radical redistribution of power and property. SV campaigns for strengthening solidarity and democracy at the expense of market forces and considers class difference and the oppression of women as structural societal problems. The party's aim is a socialist society without class difference and gender oppression, with an extended democracy in which citizens truly have equal opportunity. This basic ideological view is the backdrop for policy development in SV, particularly when it comes to the debate about the Sex Purchase Act. In SV, there is no one who has spoken for the idea that prostitution ought to be recognised as a profession or considered the result of a free choice. In line with the fundamental principles of the party, members who do not wish to penalise the purchase of sex still think that prostitution should be fought. However, the question of whether prostitution is best fought by making it illegal to buy other human beings has been the subject of a heated debate for at least two national congresses within the party. The first was held in Kristiansand in 2005, the other in Akershus in 2007. We who wished to add the criminalisation of johns to the party platform lost by a few votes in 2005, but in 2007 there was a considerable majority both in the number of votes and in people who spoke up in the debate in favour of a penalising resolution.

It is difficult to recount the story of SV's journey toward this resolution in a manner that everybody in the party will recognise and consider to be fair. A leading politician of the party, Inga Marte Thorkildsen, is among those who have put a great deal of effort into resolving these issues, and she has steadfastly campaigned against a Sex Purchase Act. She and others have emphasised that such an act will make life more difficult for prostitutes, and that the effort must instead focus on strategies to help women out of prostitution, combined with public education measures directed toward men. We who have campaigned for the legislation have pointed out that the law, first and foremost, will reduce the demand for prostitution. If men cease to buy women, fewer women will need to sell their bodies. Furthermore, the physical and psychological damage caused by a life in prostitution is so serious and extensive that it should be illegal to contribute to such hardships. Such an act also provides compensation for the violations that the prostitutes have been exposed to.

For a long time, the feminist movement in Norway has regarded prostitution as violence against women, while feminists in Germany and The Netherlands have taken entirely different positions. There are powerful forces involved in the debate about the understanding of prostitution. The debate within SV has in many ways been a tug of war between the consideration of society and the consideration of the individual. Truth be told, it is not certain that a sex purchase ban will directly help the individual prostitute if she is dependent on selling herself and does not have another alternative for income. This fact, however, does not imply acceptance of a society in which the female body is a commodity.

Pressure from the West and Wind from the North

Within SV, the campaign for banning the buying of sex was primarily driven by the party's youth organisation, Socialist Youth (*Sosialistisk Ungdom*, or SU), the regional division of the county of Hordaland, as well as parts of the women's policy committee. Besides SU and the Hordaland SV, it has largely been individuals rather than county teams that have actively agitated for the issue. I am from Norway's northernmost county, Finnmark, and I was active in the campaign against the johns who invaded our communities to purchase Russian women sold across the border after the fall of the Soviet Union.[92] The Russian peo-

---

[92] See also Chapter 4 by Marit Smuk Solbakk in this book.

ple have been in a difficult situation, beset by poverty that has caused women to leave their homes and their children in order to sell their bodies to men in Norway. Many of the women who came to Finnmark were very young, and in my immediate area they were gathered at a campsite run by a local pimp in Skiippagurra in the municipality of Tana.

There are fewer than 3,000 inhabitants in Tana, and Skiippagurra is situated a few kilometres outside of the centre, Tana Bridge. Buses filled with Russian prostitutes completely dominated the local community, and it was not long before johns and pimps met with organised resistance. The problem was that the only one who did anything illegal, according to law, was the pimp, and thus it was difficult to do anything about the problem. The situation received attention from the national media, and men came from far and wide to purchase women. Tana has probably never had as many "fishing tourists" without fishing gear as we saw at the end of the 1990s. Industrial leaders, politicians, and fathers could easily be observed at the local pub with a Russian girl on each arm, with no damaging effect on to their position in society. If they went out to have a beer, local girls were bid on as if they were up for auction, and all Russian women were branded as whores. Marriage across national borders is not an unusual phenomenon, and daughters of Russian women who were married and lived in the area became victims of harassment and verbal abuse. The impact of prostitution in the small local community created deep wounds that have not completely healed.

It is no coincidence that many of the activist forces of various parties and organisations have come from the north. The subject was brought up in several municipal councils and in the county council of Finnmark, and members campaigned for the abolition of prostitution within their respective parties. This was also the case with SV. The neighbourhood experiences with prostitution had revealed to us the futility of the legislation that existed. As long as it was legal to purchase access to another human being's body, one had to spend time advancing the political understanding of prostitution as violence against women, as well as asking men to take a stand against the violence rather than participate in it. At the same time, loopholes in the legislation needed to be searched out and closed. It was a legal action taken to prevent infections that led to the closing of the campsite of Skiippagurra, something for which the chief municipal medical doctor and feminist activist Sigrun Winterfeldt happily claim responsibility. The closing of the campsite did not bring an end to prostitution in the area. Even if the access was more difficult in Skiippagurra, the trip across the border was short.

It is not necessarily the situation in local communities that drives national politics—not when it comes to fishing administration, transport or communication, or prostitution legislation. The big cities had to get a taste of Skiippagurra through the influx of a large number of Nigerian prostitutes on the city's main streets before the public debate about criminalising johns picked up speed. It is still reasonable to ask why it took so long for a feminist party to actively engage in the campaign for the penalising of the sex buyer. SV has a different policy both for fishing administration and transport and communication than the dominant position today, so why did it take so long to assume an attitude that was similar in principle about the purchase and sale of human beings?

Pressure from the Pro-Prostitution Lobby
It is no secret that those who influenced the public debate also participated in influencing various representatives of SV in their view on this subject. At the frontline of the campaign against penalising was the Pro Centre, led by Liv Jessen. The Pro Centre describes itself as a national centre of resources and expertise within the field of prostitution, and addresses johns just as much as it addresses prostitutes. On the website of the centre, you can choose between the banners "Do You Buy Sex?" and "Do You Sell Sex?" and you are invited to a cosy chat no matter which category describes you. Under the banner "About Prostitution," prostitution is defined as the purchase and sale of sexual services and remains completely devoid of any discussion of power. The centre has instead chosen to ask leading questions such as "Is the Purchase and Sale of Sex Always About Power and Disempowerment in Society?" Beneath the same banner you can read that "few dare to tell nice stories about their experiences with prostitution" and that

prostitution assumes meaning through the frames that our culture and each of us individually set for sexuality. Our culture says that sex and love cannot possibly be bought for money. Many other countries in the world have a more pragmatic attitude toward this question than we have in Norway.

The Pro Centre campaigns to remove the stigma about prostitution, but not to remove prostitution itself. This is a very problematic viewpoint, especially in light of the centre's role and its power to establish definitions.

For a long time, the Pro Centre has claimed to be the sole authority on the environment of prostitution in the country and, further, the only ones who take the perspective of the prostitutes into consideration. The role assumed by the centre has had a major impact on the public debate and the political handling of questions regarding prostitution. I want to put forward three political consequences of the role assumed by this centre:

(1) The Pro Centre presents itself as a national centre of expertise within the field of prostitution and is therefore the only one of its kind. This implies that most of those who wish to increase their knowledge about the subject turn to them.

(2) All those who have an opinion about prostitution without assuming the attitudes of the Pro Centre are accused of attacking the prostitutes.

(3) Financial resources that are meant to help women out of prostitution are given to the Pro Centre.

The last point is perhaps the most tragic. There is a broad political majority in Norway today that wishes that prostitutes be supported in finding other ways of living and supporting themselves than selling their bodies. It is thus worthy of criticism when resources that are meant for this purpose are given to a centre that does not share such a goal. The Pro Centre describes prostitution as work and expresses in no way whatsoever that they wish to help prostitutes "change their jobs." The Centre can offer a place to get warm, someone to talk to, and free contraception. These are important measures in themselves, but they are a far cry from working systematically to help people exit prostitution.

The first two points provide, in my opinion, an explanation for why the act of criminalising the johns took such an unnecessarily long time to be passed, also within SV. A party that fights against oppression cannot act against the voice of the oppressed. If one believes the Pro Centre really speaks for prostitutes, it may seem logical to follow the advice of the centre. The centre's claim that if the johns were penalised, the prostitutes would experience even worse violence and their fear of seeking out police would increase, hit home with many members of SV. This was also an argument that made a great impression on the people who had turned to the Pro Centre in order to gain knowledge about prostitution, and who thus had trust in the centre to begin with. Among them was Inga Marte Thorkildsen, who during her time as a member of Parliament's committee on healthcare, spent several nights in the red light district in order to speak to the prostitutes. She was joined in this endeavour by representatives from the Pro Centre. It is understandable that arguments from such points of reference acquire weight.

Besides the Pro Centre, the organisation PION (the Prostitutes' Special Interest Organisation in Norway) was an actor that made the penalising question difficult for many. It is somewhat uncertain how many members PION really has, or whether it is a real special interest organisation or just a few people claiming to speak on behalf of many. In any case, representatives from PION showed up at various meetings and at the National Conferences of SV in 2005 and 2007. PION used the time very effectively by talking to delegates from different parts of the country. There are always many guests at SV's National Conferences, both from sister parties in small and large foreign countries and representatives from non-Parliament grassroots movements. They receive their invitations from the secretary of the party, hold welcoming speeches, and remind us that we have many friends in our struggle for justice and redistribution. PION, on the other hand, had invited itself.

Both the trade union movement and various parties have witnessed PION showing up and demanding to be present when prostitution and legislation is on the agenda. This has probably been an effective strategy, for most people want to listen to the groups for which the policy about to be decided will have consequences. However, prostitution is not simply a matter between the one who buys and the one who is bought. If men can legally buy access to a woman's body, this has consequences for all women. The purchase and sale of human beings speaks to the question of what kind of society we want to live in and cannot be dismissed as a private matter between those who are directly involved. This is also an understanding that is well established within most other political questions. Few have, for example, spoken up for refugees' right to define refugee policy, but the debate about penalisation of johns is governed by completely different guidelines. Suddenly, it was more important than ever to have the involved parties present, despite the fact that the special interest organisation PION in no way shared SV's feminist principles. This has also been the problem: while the Pro Centre and, to some degree, PION are dominating voices, they are heard even by parties and organisations that do not share their fundamental beliefs. I am not in any way saying that one can only listen and talk to organisations and individuals who are of the same opinion as oneself, but a common understanding ought to be fundamental if one chooses to follow advice. I would, for example, invite children in childcare and child welfare officers rather than abusive parents if there were to be a revision of the Child Welfare Act.

The Pressure from the Youth

Socialist Youth (SU) has been agitating for the penalising position in SV. I was on the central board of SU from 2002 to 2008 and spent the last two years as a leader. SU adopted the position in 2000, but the question had already come up for debate in 1998. Then the result was a majority by a single vote to pursue the criminalisation of johns. Thus, the question had every right to be discussed again at SU's National Conference in 2000, and has since been a part of the youth organisation's feminist schooling and political focus. Many SU members took part in the public discussion of the question. In addition to writing newspaper contributions, holding actions, and engaging in debates, many representatives in SU did solid work to promote the debate in their SV home counties. Political schooling and conscious focus made it possible for SU to push the matter at the National Congresses of 2005 and 2007.

For SU, one of the political agenda items for the SV National Conference in 2007 was that the party should take a stand for the penalising of johns. The majority had been rather scant two years earlier and, in addition, the political situation had been entirely different. The capital had had a taste of Skiippagurra. More people noticed and had to confront the fact of prostitution when the number of foreign prostitutes exploded on Karl Johan, the city's main street. Earlier, women had sold themselves on the side streets, but now they suddenly invaded the street where tourists and visitors get their first impression of our country. On top of that, many of the prostitutes were from Nigeria and were therefore particularly visible. The same thing that had happened in Finnmark 10 years earlier was now being repeated in Oslo: African girls stayed at home during the evenings because they were bid for when they went out for a drink. In the same way that all Russian women had been branded as whores, black women now felt the daily harassment. Prostitution also increased noticeably in Trondheim, Bergen, and Stavanger. The question of criminalising the johns thus acquired an entirely new reality just before the National Conference of SV in 2007. More groups took a stand regarding the question, and a short time before the National Conference, the police offered opinions in support of changes in the legislation.

National Congress Thriller

It was challenging to campaign for a breakthrough in favour of a sex purchase ban, because unlike with other political questions, it was now less obvious who thought what. It was clear that most people did not define the question on a right-left axis. SU worked systematically to ally themselves with those who shared their ideas and whose opinions were very important within the party, and by sending out youth to discuss the case in the various counties prior to the National Congress. During the congress, we urged as many as possible to speak out in favour of penalisation. The arguments were many and included the points that prostitution is violence against women and that the physical and psychological damage of being in prostitution is well documented. Therefore, one must see the resolution as connected to SV's general campaign against violence against women. A society cannot be equalised as long as men, with the law in hand, can purchase access to women's bodies. Also, legislation influences attitudes about what is acceptable in society, and attitudes determine actions. It is the customer who should be held responsible for the existence of and increase in prostitution; if no one had wanted to buy access to other people's bodies, no one would have needed to sell their bodies. Therefore, the customer must be held responsible and punished. With such a law in place, the police would possess the means by which to battle prostitution.

These arguments were at the core of many of the contributions, and we who pushed for criminalisation dominated the debate at the National Congress of 2007. I still believed that the battle was lost when party leader Kristin Halvorsen summarised the debate about the political situation, saying that the suggestion to add the criminalisation of johns to our statement had been heavily debated, among other things. The party leader made an effort to talk about conversations she had had with prostitutes and how frightened they were of the police to begin with. I remember her saying something like, "we cannot support political resolutions that will make life for prostitutes even more difficult." Kristin is good at speaking to people's hearts, and she has an ability to appeal to the sense of justice most people have about the things that are most difficult. She also made the point that caused many to be uncertain: the opinions about how the ban had worked in Sweden were quite different, and both sides put forth statistics and stories to support their views.

The joy was enormous when the voting showed a clear majority supporting the criminalisation of johns. The statement was very clear-cut, both regarding the perspective of power that made the clients responsible as well as the measures to take in order to help prostitutes find new ways of making a living. In the period 2005-2013 SV partook in a governmental coallition with the Labour Party and the Centre Party. When SV decided to support the sex purchase ban in 2007, it was not just about a feminist party taking a wise stand. It was also about what the ruling policy of the country should be.

The Fight to Criminalise the Purchase of Sex: An Icelandic Fighting Saga

Kolbrún Halldórsdóttir

In the 1990s, when Sweden passed new legislation called *Kvinnofrid* on sexual violence and the abolition of gendered discrimination, the fight for similar legislation began in Iceland. Later on, the Swedes criminalised the purchase of sexual favours with the introduction of the Sex Purchase Act no. 408/1998. The grassroots sector of the women's movement was the first to call the attention of Icelandic politicians to the new Swedish law. They organised symposia on sexual violence against women and held meetings with the politicians in order to discuss potential improvements for the Icelandic legislation.

So what was the situation when the fight started? The first strip club in Iceland opened its doors in 1995, but it was soon followed by others. By the year 2000, there were twelve strip clubs: eight in Reykjavík, three in Akureyri, and one in Keflavík. Most of the women dancing at the clubs were of foreign origin, and in 1999 around 1,000 women were believed to have been imported to Iceland in order to be exploited in the clubs. The police kept a sharp eye on these places, as they were suspected of engaging in illegal activities such as prostitution and drug dealing. This suspicion was substantiated by the fact that the clubs offered private dancing: the customer would buy access to a room where he could be alone with a naked woman.

Before long, the strip clubs were also suspected of being involved in trafficking. Minister of Justice Sólveig Pétursdóttir, from the Independence Party, was quoted as saying that a consulate from an

Eastern European state had been contacted by women complaining that they had been enticed to come to Iceland under false pretenses. The women believed that they were going to work at restaurants, when in reality they were all meant to engage in prostitution. The minister requested her fellow countrymen to be on guard regarding this kind of international crime and declared herself willing to participate fully in the international measures that had to be taken to stop trafficking. Nevertheless, it proved difficult for the minister to garner support for her views in the government and in the Icelandic Parliament (the Althingi).

It was the women working at Stígamót, a guidance and information centre for women and children who were victims of sexual violence, as well as the women working at the crisis centre in Reykjavík, who were the first to inform the public of the realities they witnessed. They said that more and more women sought them out because of the serious consequences of a life in prostitution. Women sought shelter at the centre from violent Icelandic husbands who had imported them through the "mail-order bride" companies. The rights of these women had not been discussed previously in the Icelandic media, and the idea of prostitution as violence against women was completely new in Iceland.

It was obvious that the women performing in the Icelandic strip clubs came from Eastern Europe. During a UN conference concerned with women and democracy held in Reykjavík in 1999, the Icelandic people were amazed when Lithuanian President Vaira Vike-Freiberga urgently requested that the states of the world stop all trafficking in human beings. The president's appeal came across loud and clear: the time had come for the Western states to come together and find a way to prevent this slave market from continuing. The Swedes had already started, and the question now was: Which nations had the courage to follow their lead?

This chapter focuses on the fight to criminalise the purchase of sexual favours in Iceland—a fight that led to the introduction of a Sex Purchase Act that was passed by the Icelandic Parliament on April 17, 2009, with 27 votes for and 3 against, with 16 abstentions. Until then, the Icelandic law had banned prostitution with the intention to support oneself, and the maximum penalty had been 24 months' imprisonment.

The law had very rarely been enforced, and never in the Supreme Court - probably because of the law's condition that prostitution had to be a means to support oneself, and especially because the law gave no definition of how large a part of one's income should stem from prostitution in order to reach criminal status. Until 1992, provisions on prostitution fell under the laws on income and work habits.

This chapter touches only on the period after Sweden introduced the criminalisation of the purchase of sexual favours. After the Swedish law was passed in 1999, Kristín Ástgeirsdóttir, from the Women's List, asked the Minister of Justice whether the current government knew if there were indications of a systematic importation of foreign women, especially from Eastern Europe, and—regarding the Swedish amendments—if the minister believed that there was a basis for changing the law. The minister replied that a systematic study of the extent of prostitution had not been carried out, but it was rumoured that prostitution was connected to strip clubs. The rumours had, however, not been confirmed, and the government had made no decisions about amendments to fight the threat of prostitution.

The minister's reply precipitated a 10-year fight in the Althingi about following the Swedish example and introducing a legal sex-purchase ban. The fight really began in the winter of 1999–2000 when Þuríður Backman and I, both representing the Left-Green Movement, made a proposal concerning a change in the penal code no. 19/1940. During the 1980s, members of the Althingi from the Women's List had called attention to the need for a change in the public attitude toward prostitution. In the winter of 1991–1992, when the Althingi read a proposal from the government about changing the penal code's chapter on sexual crimes, Anna Ólafsdóttir Björnsson and Ingibjörg Sólrún Gísladóttir from the Women's List offered an amendment about reducing criminal liability for women supporting themselves through prostitution. The amendment was defeated by three-fourths of the votes.

In the proposal that Þuríður and I made on March 7, 2000, it was not only proposed that the criminal liability for the person supporting himself/herself through prostitution should be removed, but it was also suggested that the there should be a shift in criminal liability, that is, that it should be placed on the sex buyer. The proposal also contained changes in relation to pornography and strip shows, as we wanted to call attention to Iceland's changed reality—for example, the growing number of strip clubs and the indications of criminal activity linked to the clubs.

The proposal was not read that year but still received quite a lot of attention in the media. There was much discussion, especially concerning whether it would be inappropriate to limit the number of strip clubs or perhaps even ban them completely. Two positions emerged. The right wing believed that the clubs should not be banned, as they clearly met a demand, and at a debate meeting held by the Independence Party's youth organisation in November 1999, the idea was expressed that the public debate was manipulated and distorted. This was to be expected, they said, seeing as the feminists fronted the issue, and their handling of the case was characterised by prejudice and a lack of knowledge. Members of the Althingi were criticised for their lack of objectivity, since their reasoning was built on groundless rumours. Þorgerður Katrín Gunnarsdóttir, deputy chairman of the Independence Party and later Minister of Teaching, Research, and Culture, believed that it was unrealistic to ban the strip clubs, but that it was important to find out whether the women had chosen their jobs of their own free will. She criticised the fact that the women had not been asked to apply for a work permit, but according to the law at the time, artists did not need a work permit. (This provision was changed a few years later.) Þorgerður Katrín was also critical of the fact that the women had been exempt from health controls.

The media took great pains to explain the difference between those who engaged in prostitution out of need and those who engaged in it voluntarily. One could say that it was around this time that the myth of "the happy hooker" began. This myth persisted until the spring of 2003, when the movie *Lilya 4-ever*, by Swedish film director Lucas Moodyson, was shown in Iceland. The film, which told the story of a young woman being trafficked into prostitution, had a huge influence on public opinion.

The discussion about strip clubs moved into the Althingi during the winter of 1999–2000, when the Minister of Communication made a proposal regarding the classification of restaurants, in which night-clubs should have a special classification, with strip clubs as a subgroup. The minister and the government were criticised for the proposal, and several claimed that it made stripping a legal occupation in Iceland, something that was unacceptable, considering the indications that prostitution was linked to these clubs. Jón Bjarnason from the Left-Green Movement offered an amendment that meant that the concept of striptease as an occupation was not used in the law. The Minister of Communication's proposal was defeated 32 votes to 3. It was therefore partly up to the local authorities to give licenses to strip clubs, which again resulted in many conflicts with the municipalities.

In the spring of 2000, the law regarding work permits for coun-trymen of foreign origin changed. Unlike artists on a temporary visit, women who performed at the strip clubs were no longer granted an exemption from the rules concerning work permits. This change re-sulted in fewer women coming from countries outside the EU; instead, women already working in strip clubs within the European Economic Area (EEA) began to arrive in Iceland. Thus, the change in the law had exerted no influence on the strip clubs and their management. A fight loomed in the Althingi as well as in the municipalities. Radical changes were needed in order to close down the strip clubs.

The women from Stígamót, under the leadership of Guðrún Jónsdóttir, had campaigned tirelessly and courageously to make the public aware of how serious the consequences were for women in pros-titution. Stígamót urgently requested that purchasing sexual favours should be categorised as sexual violence against women and as per-petration of that violence, where the responsibility rests with the sex buyer or john. This was based on the belief that the john in the situation is the more powerful party and that he is the one with an actual choice as to whether he should buy or not buy sex.

The women from Stígamót wanted the different women's organ-isations to stand together. They held debate meetings and tried their best to give the nation food for thought concerning pornography, prostitution, and human trafficking. They made a poster and published it as an ad in newspapers and periodicals. It attracted huge attention because it showed a number of women lying in a meat tray, wrapped up in plastic and looking like chicken wings. Everybody immediately got the message: the population had to stand up to the unpleasant fact that in Iceland, women's bodies were for sale. Those who advocated for the Swedish model in the Althingi borrowed the arguments of the women's movement and emphasised the link between pornography, prostitution, and trafficking. They emphasised as well that a result would only be achieved in the fight against trafficking—which most members in the Althingi supported—if, at the same time, Iceland fought against the pornography and prostitution industry.

At the beginning of 2001, I again made a proposal concerning the purchase of sexual favours. The general committee submitted the proposal to a hearing, but the statements arrived too late to be included in the reading of the proposal before the Althingi went on holiday. However, there were other possibilities for keeping the issue on the front burner. The UN's Palermo Protocols were ready in 2000, and they had been signed on behalf of the Icelandic government. I posed a question as to whether the government had any plans to introduce the provisions of the protocols, and the Minister of Justice, Sólveig Pétursdóttir, was sympathetic to the question, but this was not enough. Another six years were to pass before the Althingi voted for the proposal of Foreign Minister Sólrún Gísladóttir to ratify the Palermo Protocols.

In 2001, Stígamót organised a conference for the network Nordic Women Against Violence under the title "The Unyielding Assailant." During the conference, one of the things that the participants talked about was the Swedish legislation, which at the time had been in force for two and a half years. At the end of the conference, the participants agreed on a declaration that pointed out that prostitution is ultimately a form of violence against women, and the Nordic governments were therefore requested to follow the Swedish example and criminalise the purchase of sexual favours. That way, the responsibility for the violence was moved from the victims of the violence to the perpetrators;

moreover, it sent a clear signal that it is unacceptable that women and children's bodies are for sale.

The fact that pornography, prostitution, and trafficking were discussed much more in the Althingi resulted in growing media coverage of prostitution and related matters, at the same time that the media reported more often about young people who financed their drug addictions through prostitution. The growing awareness was also due to the fact that in 2001, two different studies on prostitution were published. One of them was built on a survey in Iceland, and the other compared the different Nordic laws on pornography and prostitution. In the spring of 2001, the Minister of Justice set up a committee charged with the task of making proposals about how to respond to the conclusions of the two studies. The committee made its proposals in April 2002 and recommended that it should no longer be a punishable offence to sell sexual favours to support oneself, but it would be acceptable to levy fines against people if they offered sexual favours in public. The committee, however, did not believe that the time had come to criminalise the purchase of sexual favours.

It is likely that the proposal that Minister of Justice Pétursdóttir made in the autumn of 2001 about penalising the purchase of sexual favours from children under the age of 18 resulted from the pressure following the widespread public discussion in the spring and summer of that year. Furthermore, the proposal stated that the importation and possession of child pornography should be punished more severely. Judging from the reaction to the proposal, further amendments could be expected concerning the legal protection of children and youngsters in connection with sexual crimes. Nevertheless, the minister never answered the questions posed to her in the debate as to whether the government was ready to take a closer look at the Swedish model and criminalise the purchase of sexual favours from adults as well.

The town council in Reykjavík was clearly affected by the debate, and in March 2003 the police regulation in Reykjavík was changed such that private dancing in strip clubs was banned. The ban was met with mixed feelings and was submitted to be tried in court. In the end, the Supreme Court confirmed the powers of the town council. Many municipalities followed—indeed, many wanted to go even further by completely banning strip clubs, but in order to do so the law needed to be changed. The municipalities viewed a change favourably, but the law sided with the club owners, and the fight continued for a number of years.

The debate changed during the winter of 2002–2003 when the government finally adopted an amendment that specified trafficking as a criminal offence. The general committee put a great deal of work into the matter, which also consisted of important provisions concerning sexual crimes against children. These included better legal protection for children between the ages of 16 to 18, as well as stronger sentences for sexual crimes committed against children. The government was criticised at the first reading of the proposal for not having stepped up the process and criminalising the purchase of sexual favours. It was evident that the Swedish law had had the effect that human traffickers who dealt with trafficking in prostitution no longer regarded Sweden as a desirable trade area. After an exhaustive review in the general committee, the committee submitted a joint report for the second reading in the Althingi urgently requesting the government to ratify the Palermo Protocols as soon as possible. During the second reading of the proposal, I made an amendment stating that the purchase of sexual favours should be penalised in the same way as the selling of sexual favours. The amendment was defeated 27 to 9. This was the first time the Icelandic Althingi had had the opportunity to vote for a criminalisation of the purchase of sexual favours, but it was not to be the last.

In June 2003, the women from Stígamót organised an interesting conference in Reykjavík at which a European organisation, the European Network Against Trafficking in Women for Sexual Exploitation, met to discuss the selling of women for sexual slavery. It caused a media sensation when a Greek speaker said that the city council in Athens planned to build more brothels in connection with the Olympic Games in 2004, for the reason that the council wanted to take into account the growing demand for prostitutes during the games. The participants at the conference immediately released a statement in which they emphatically criticised the International Olympic Committee for planning pornography and violence alongside the Olympic Games, as this was a direct contravention of the UN's articles regarding prostitution and trafficking—areas in which humiliation, wretchedness, and the infringement of human rights were prevalent. The news about the building plans in Athens definitely played a role in the discussion about the purchase of sexual favours in Iceland. The news had also reached the Nordic and Baltic Ministers of Equal Opportunities, who released a joint statement regarding the case—all except the Danish Minister, Henriette Kjær, who saw no reason to protest.

In the autumn of 2003, a number of Icelandic women's organisations invited the Swedish Minister of Equal Opportunities at the time, Margareta Winberg, to Iceland to give a speech on the Swedish gender discrimination act called *Kvinnofrid* and also the Swedish model. Her visit received a lot of media coverage and was a boost for the new Althingi, which had been elected earlier that year. The work of the Althingi was also influenced by the fact that 14 women's organisations submitted a proclamation to the members of Parliament that urged them to criminalise the purchase of sexual favours when the Althingi assembled in the autumn. The 14 organisations were the Feminist Society of Iceland, Bríet (young feminists), Icelandic Women's Societies, the Crisis Centre, the Women's Church, the Guidance Centre for Women, the Society for Women's Rights, the Emergency Reception for Rape Victims, Stígamót, the periodical *Vera*, UNIFEM in Iceland, the Organisation of Women Doctors, Women in the Progressive Party, and V-Day in Iceland. The statement following the proclamation emphasised the link between the pornography industry and prostitution and pointed out that prostitution should be regarded as a form of violence against women that must be fought. Introducing a criminalisation of the purchase of sexual favours would further the fight.

In hindsight, when summarising the fight against sexual violence against women, the efforts of the women's movement—specifically, the efforts of the 14 organisations mentioned earlier who signed the declaration that was sent to the members of the Althingi—stand out clearly. However, the women from Stígamót were particularly active in the fight. At the frontlines of battle, one would find Stígamót's leader,

Guðrún Jónsdóttir, who had worked earlier in Norway building and strengthening the work of the Nordic Women against sexual violence against women. Guðrún knew the women researchers in the area as well as the competent activists from our neighbouring countries, and she invited them as often as possible to participate in symposia and conferences about prostitution and trafficking. Among these women were Dorit Otzen from Denmark, who has worked with prostitutes for many decades; Janice G. Raymond from America, who represented the Coalition Against Trafficking in Women; Gunilla Ekberg from Sweden, who is the appointed expert for the Swedish government in prostitution and trafficking; Marit Kvamme from the Norwegian Women's Front, who had called for solidarity in the fight against prostitution and trafficking in Norway; Margareta Winberg, the Swedish Minister of Equal Opportunities, and many others.

During the 2003 elections, the prostitution debate was not very visible, and the result of the election provided little hope that the government would change their view in regard to the Swedish model. The Independence Party and the Progressive Party kept their majority, and after the election, Iceland got a new Minister of Justice, Björn Bjarnason, from the Independence Party. Once again, a proposal was made for the criminalisation of the purchase of sexual favours. This time, we were 14 members, representing four political parties, who made the proposal— and all were women. We represented the Left-Green Movement, the Social Democratic Alliance, the Progressive Party, and the Liberal Party—in other words, all of the women in the Althingi except for the women from the Independence Party. Unfortunately, the debate in Parliament focused a great deal on the allegations coming from the women of the Independence Party, who claimed that the persons making the proposal had it out for the women of the Independence Party.

That winter, the general committee spent a great deal of time reading the proposal, as well as another proposal that I had initiated about the protection of victims and witnesses in cases of trafficking. Among those summoned by the general committee was the Swedish anthropologist Petra Östergren. She had just finished her MA thesis in anthropology, in which she dealt with the conditions of prostitutes in Sweden, and the youth organisation of the Independence Party (SUS) had therefore invited her to Iceland. At the same time, the 14 women's organisations mentioned earlier had invited a Swedish police officer, Thomas Ekman. He was the head of the police team working with prostitution and trafficking in women in Göteborg, and he was also summoned by the committee for a meeting. The two Swedes had very different views of the Swedish model, and their visit was symbolic of the fight between the different views in Iceland.

Only a few days remained in the parliamentary session in spring 2004 when an attempt was made to make the general committee put the finishing touches on the case. A new majority had assembled for this proposal in the committee, and representatives from all political parties except the Independence Party agreed to send the proposal to the Althingi. They submitted a report recommending that Parliament vote in favour of the proposal. This newly acquired power provoked the anger of the Independence Party, since they opposed adding the proposal to the agenda. A fight broke out in the chairmanship of the Althingi, and the Independence Party, together with the Althingi's chairman and Minister of Justice Björn Bjarnason, won. The result was that the proposal was not added to the agenda.

Well before the Althingi reconvened in the autumn of 2004, I tried to get the women in the Independence Party to participate in the majority, made up of parliamentary members who now were in favour of repealing the law that made it a criminal offence to offer sexual favours for payment and instead held the johns responsible. The women in the Independence Party did not want a repetition of what had happened in the autumn of 2003. Therefore, they suggested that the Minister of Justice, Björn Bjarnason, set up a committee whose task would be to familiarise themselves with experiences of the Swedish law, as well as take a close look at the laws and the debates about prostitution in the other Nordic countries. Furthermore, they wanted us to hold back on making the proposal until the committee had presented its conclusions, and I agreed to do so. On November 23, 2004, the Minister of Justice set up a committee consisting of parliamentary members from all the political parties in order to examine legislation on prostitution, the porn industry, and trafficking in Europe. The committee finished its work a year later and presented its report in February 2006. I kept my word and shelved the proposal while the committee worked.

In the spring of 2006, Minister of Justice Björn Bjarnason introduced a proposal concerning a complete revision of the penal code's chapter on sexual crimes no.19/1940. Since the parliamentary session was coming to an end, it was clear that the work would not be finished in time, and the proposal was therefore made once again when the Althingi assembled in the fall. The author of the proposal was Ragnheiður Bragadóttir, Professor of Law at the University of Iceland. Finally, a proposal was made to decriminalise the selling of sexual favours, but the proposal did not go so far as to suggest the criminalisation of the purchase of sexual favours. The grounds for the proposal were long and detailed, as the politicians did not want to risk being accused of wanting to legalise prostitution, and a new provision was introduced that banned the creation of public advertisements for prostitution. The feminist movement sharply criticised this viewpoint.

When the proposal went to the general committee, something unexpected happened that influenced public opinion and, thus, the further development of the case. In mid-July, we received news that pornography producers on the Internet were to meet in Iceland and hold a conference described as "Snowgathering." About 200 visitors had registered, and among these were some famous porn stars whose photographs were going to be taken in the Icelandic landscape. The visitors were going to stay at the Radisson SAS, a hotel owned by the Icelandic Farmer Organisation. Led by the women from Stígamót, the feminist movement formed a united front and requested that the town council prevent the conference from being held, because the movement was of the opinion that it was necessary to fight pornification and prostitution. The mayor then declared that those kinds of conferences were not welcome, and that the town council did not want Reykjavík to become the home of pornography producers, considering the fact that the production and possession of pornography is banned according to Icelandic law. The members of the Althingi were invited to meet the activists, who demanded that they take a stand on the issue. The Icelandic bishop and the chairman of the clergymen's association strongly condemned the conference, and the blogs were in flames on the Internet. When the female activists started sending Internet links to the politicians, the media, and the police showing the activities of the producers behind the conference, it became clear that the porn conference would not see the light of day in Iceland.

Finally, the owners of the hotel, the Icelandic Farmer Organisation, cancelled their agreement with the pornography producers, who threatened to claim damages for financial losses. No more was heard from the pornography producers, but public opinion had clearly shifted in favour of those who wanted to fight the pornification of society. Moreover, there seemed to be a greater understanding of the fact that the porn industry, prostitution, and trafficking were all connected. This was revealed in an opinion poll carried out shortly after the incident in which the public was asked their opinion on the criminalisation of the purchase of sexual favours.

The incident influenced the Althingi's general committee, and when their statement about the penal code's chapter on sexual crimes was submitted on March 14, there was general agreement across party lines regarding the main points of the proposal. Nevertheless, the opposition, consisting of the Social Democratic Alliance and the Left-Green Movement, offered an amendment concerning some important points—for example, the purchase of sexual favours could be subject to a fine or 12 months' imprisonment. They had also suggested that sexual crimes against children be exempt from the provision concerning the period of limitation. The fight over these points was an arduous one, but it went on behind closed doors. The Independence Party was determined to prevent the proposal from being put to a vote, since the majority would vote for it. After various meetings and different offers from all parties, the opposition's amendment was finally passed: sexual crimes against children were, on the whole, exempt from the period of limitation and, from now on, they were exempt from the law of limitation. Apart from that, two important issues were resolved in the general committee, one of them about the protection of victims of trafficking, and the other about the right of the police to remove violent men from their homes if they were a danger to others in the home. For the time being, we had to be content with the passage of these points, whereas the proposal on the criminalisation of the purchase of sexual favours was not put to a vote. My reaction to this was to distribute a proposal on the criminalisation of the purchase of sexual favours on the last working day of the parliamentary session as a declaration of the continuing fight.

On this last day, the Althingi voted in favour of a new law concerning restaurants, hotels, and entertainment in which striptease was banned in restaurants, with the exception that the people who gave the license could allow striptease if the licensee had received positive evaluations from rapporteurs. It was pointed out that even though the licensee had received a licence and thereby an exemption from the law, the dancers were not allowed to go out among the audience, and all types of private dancing were banned. This result was unsatisfactory to many members of Parliament, and they announced that they would continue the fight for a total ban on strip clubs.

After the spring elections, the Independence Party and the Social Democratic Alliance formed a government, and yet again a proposal was made on the criminalisation of the purchase of sexual favours. This time the proposal was made by members of the Althingi representing three political parties: the Left-Green Movement, the Social Democratic Alliance, and the Progressive Party. When the proposal was taken up for general discussion in January 2008, only two members from the Althingi participated—Minister of Justice Björn Bjarnason and myself. Among other things, Bjarnason believed that the results of the Swedish model had not been that positive, and he quoted the research carried out by Petra Östergren. I countered by presenting the study mentioned earlier that had been conducted in the spring of the same year, which showed that a large contingent of the Icelandic people supported the Swedish model. The study showed that 70% of the population were in favour of the criminalisation of the purchase of sexual favours, including 82.5% of the women of Iceland and 57.1% of the men.

The Social Democratic Alliance now formed the government, and one could sense that change was about to come when cases concerning trafficking were moved from Björn Bjarnason's Ministry of Justice to the Ministry of Social Affairs headed by Jóhanna Sigurðardóttir. On January 22, 2008, Jóhanna set up a committee whose task was to make a proposal for a plan regarding the prevention of trafficking in Iceland. Furthermore, the Minister of Foreign Affairs and party leader of the Social Democratic Alliance, Ingibjörg Sólrún Gísladóttir, motioned for a resolution on the ratification of the Palermo Protocols. The resolution was passed, and the preparations to make the necessary amendments in order to ratify the Palermo Protocols began immediately after.

Even though a large part of the discussion in the Althingi focused on the financial situation, the Left-Green Movement made a proposal about prostitution and trafficking. Earlier the same year, some members of Parliament introduced a bill calling for change in the new law on restaurants, hotels, and entertainment. They suggested that the exception covering striptease should be removed and that the ban should be without exception. The bill was read and sent to the general committee, where it was shelved.

I made the proposal again in the autumn, this time together with members from the Social Democratic Alliance and the Progressive Party, and we expected to have the majority on our side. We did not expect the case to get any attention, as it was during the banking crisis, and people were protesting in great numbers outside the Althingi—protests that led to the government's resignation. When that happened at the end of January 2009, the Social Democratic Alliance and the Left-Green Movement formed a minority government with the support of the Progressive Party.

The time had come to follow through on some of the cases that the Independence Party had opposed, and as I had now become a minister in the new government, it was more suitable for others to make the proposals. The documents were changed, and Siv Friðleifsdóttir from the Progressive Party took over. On March 12, 2009, she made a proposal that the exception concerning striptease licensing should be deleted from the law. This time, the reading in the general committee went fast, and the report, which recommended passage of the proposal, was ready on March 30th. That the committee members from the Independence

Party signed the report attracted attention, even though it was with a reservation. Nevertheless, the case was still not settled because of the public demand for a new election, as well as immense pressure on the members of Parliament, and the proposal never made it to a third reading.

The election for the Althingi was held on April 26, 2009, and the Social Democratic Alliance, along with the Left-Green Movement, received a clear mandate from the voters to form a government. The government came to power on May 10, 2009, and 10 days later, Siv Friðleifsdóttir, together with parliamentary members from all political parties, once again made the proposal concerning a total ban on strip-tease. The legal ban against strip clubs was passed in the Althingi on Tuesday, March 23, 2010.

Take a Stand, Man!

Hanne Helth

On an ice-cold winter's night at the beginning of the new millennium, I was visiting a northern Finnish brothel camp with Russian prostitutes. When the women saw our car arriving, they came running out of their huts and stood in the frosty weather, wearing nothing but g-strings and bras behind a barbed-wire fence and a gate through which only sex buyers were allowed to pass. Their pimps beat us with cudgels until we fled. It is one of the strong images that I will always carry with me: the fenced-in, almost-naked women in the frosty weather.

In my 20 years as a social worker among marginalised groups, I have never experienced the amount of violence and misery with which I was confronted after starting to work in the area of prostitution. On my travels to many Western and Eastern European countries, I talked with prostitutes in brothels, in backyards, on the streets, in the woods, and at hotels. Everywhere I was met with the same cynicism, wretchedness, and denial. I will spare you the details of the many horrifying accounts about women being exposed to battering by johns and pimps. Prostitution destroyed people's lives and robbed them of the few remaining options they might have had. All the while, johns rushed past me with the greatest of ease. It seemed to be a law of nature that some men bought sex, and that they had a right to do so. Buying sex took place in such a manner that it was visible to everybody who might take the trouble to look for it. In most countries, nobody raises an eyebrow, even though the many damaging effects that prostitutes suffer from because of a life in prostitution are well known. Nobody raises an eyebrow, even though members of the society have to live with the structural disparity that buying sex expresses.

I have never understood, and never will understand, how it is possible for johns to ignore the fact that they, through their sexual actions, risk destroying the life of another human being. When I stopped my activities as a social worker, the numerous images of violence and ruined lives did not cease to torture my gaze. In Denmark, prostitution was growing, and society turned a blind eye to it. The Danish debate on prostitution was based on myths and focused primarily on the conditions of the victims of trafficking. From time to time there was some attention paid to Danish women engaged in prostitution, as well as the people who profited from the prostitution of others—pimps, traffickers, and so on. Even so, the third party involved in prostitution—the sex buyer—was non-existent in the public mind; he was not included in the debate on prostitution. On the contrary, since I began my outreach casework among street prostitutes in Copenhagen, the john seemed to me to be everywhere. He is the ordinary lecherous man with money and power, who thinks that it is quite all right to satisfy his lechery when it suits him, and in the manner that suits him best, by paying for sex, irrespective of the consequences for the person selling it to him.

In order to reduce the exploitation of human beings in prostitution, it is imperative that the responsibility and actions of the sex buyers become visible to the public. This is why the john has to be exposed—he who is responsible for the growth in prostitution and trafficking, he who had been invisible in the Danish debate on prostitution, and he whom I constantly ran into in my outreach casework.

Prostitution is the most serious and systematic exploitation of human beings—primarily women and children—taking place all over the world. Prostitution affects the poor, the sexually abused, and the outcast, and it primarily affects the daughters and sons of the working class and the classless. But the enormous social imbalance along the lines of gender, class, and ethnicity is evident only on the supply side. When it comes to the demand side, the picture is completely different: no matter the sex, class, or nationality of the person being bought, it is men who buy sex, and they come from all classes, nationalities, occupational and marital backgrounds, and so on. Several studies have shown that these factors are closely connected to each other.[93] Thus, prostitution is all about the way some men manage their sexuality, power, and money. The sex buyers are at the very core of all prostitution, and most societies want to hide this fact. The john is the invisible man who finances the entire sex industry, trafficking in women, different mafias, and so forth. Most societies believe that prostitution is necessary for men's survival, and they stubbornly maintain that idea—as if men would drop dead if they did not have the option of paying a woman to achieve sexual satisfaction. When you think of it, it is actually a rather comic idea; as the Danish scholar of masculinity Kenneth Reinicke incisively remarks: "No man has yet dropped dead from having an erect penis!"

From a global perspective, one can see that the lack of opportunity for women to provide for themselves, their children, and the elderly, to own land or real property, to be protected against violence and war— simply a lack of avenues for self-determination—stands in direct proportion to the extent of the sex industry in a given country. If the oppression of women in a society is so strong that no women's movement exists to demand women's liberation, the sex industry is given free rein to expand in size as well as in power. If the women's movement fails to mount a strong and organised resistance to the exploitation of human beings in prostitution, there will be no limit to the extent of prostitution and trafficking. Instead, some countries will fully legalise the sex industry, resulting in an explosive growth in prostitution and trafficking. In addressing the question of whether prostitution can be combated or not, the strength and power of the women's movement to define prostitution as sexual exploitation is paramount.

---

[93] For example, *Challenging men's demand for prostitution in Scotland: A research report based on interviews with 110 men who bought women in prostitution*, McLeod, Farley, Anderson and Golding, 2008; *Men who buy sex: Who they buy and what they know*, Farley, Bindel and Golding, 2009; and *Det skal ikke bare være en krop mod krop oplevelse*, Lautrup, VFC Socialt Udsatte, 2005 (not translated into English).

Prostitution in Denmark

Throughout the last two decades, the number of prostitutes and broth-els in Denmark has grown dramatically. In 1999, earning money through prostitution was decriminalised. According to figures from public au-thorities, there were 466 brothels in 2009,[94] whereas public figures on the number of prostitutes have varied from 5,400 to 7,800[95] in 2002; to 5,521[96] in 2009; to a minimum estimate of 3,483 in 2011.[97] The variation in the figures is partly political, partly methodological, and partly due to the hidden nature of the sex industry. About half of the prostitutes are of foreign origin and are therefore especially dependent upon pimps and traffickers because they earn a living as prostitutes in a foreign country. However, the rise in prostitution cannot be explained simply by an increase in the number of foreign women engaged in it. For the math to make sense, it must mean that more Danish women end up in prostitution, compared to the situation 15 or 20 years ago.

Studies carried out by the Danish National Board of Social Services (*Servicestyrelsen*) show that people involved in prostitution often lack training or have only short-cycle training, and there is a predominance of people that have experienced sexual assaults in their childhood.[98] A major reason for becoming a prostitute is a poor financial situation, often combined with a lack of recognition of one's own worth—for ex-ample, when johns pay childhood sexual abuse victims for sex, it helps to ease low self-esteem. Depending upon the form of prostitution, a Danish survey shows that between 60% and 95% of the prostitutes are exposed either to violence or threats of violence, and that 30% have

---

[94] *Beskrivelse af politiets indsats mod prostitutionens bagmænd 2009*, http://www.politi. dk/NR/rdonlyres/EA7AD422-5E04-4B47-886A-84D86D45AD74/0/Beskrivelseafpoli tietsindsatsmodprostbagm%C3%A6nd2009.pdf

[95] *PRO-centerets årsberetning 2001*

[96] *Prostitution i Danmark—årsrapport 2009*, http://www.servicestyrelsen.dk/ udgivelser/udsatte/prostitution/prostitution-i-danmark-arsrapport-2009

[97] The figures are taken from the Danish National Board of Social Services, *Notat om prostitutionens omfang og former 2010*, http://www.servicestyrelsen.dk/udgivelser/ udsatte/prostitution/prostitutionens-omfang-og-former-notat

[98] See the reports from the Danish National Board of Social Services, *Prostitution i Danmark* (2007), *Prostitutionens omfang of former* (2008) as well as the report from Kompetencecenter Prostitution *Aspekter ved prostitution* (2009) and their web page, www.kcprostitution.dk/page688.asp

been raped.[99] Prostitutes are, to a large extent, moulded by their experiences, which may lead to difficulties such as holding down an ordinary job, getting an education, and becoming independent. They may also find it hard to take on a parental role or become emotionally attached to their partner because of emotional damage from a life in prostitution. The damage stemming from prostitution is part of an ongoing destructive process that, in many cases, is only realised and felt later on—years after one has stopped prostituting.

A Danish study from 2005 concerning men who buy sex shows that 14% of all Danish men—about 300,000 men—have bought sex once or several times in their lives.[100] One-third of these, or about 100,000 men, are what we might describe as habitual sex buyers. The johns are usually quite ordinary men: the largest group is in a relationship or married, and only 8% seem to think that they have no other option but to buy sex from prostitutes. Most johns explain that they buy sex because it is readily accessible and that society does not frown upon it. The Danish prostitution market is very well organised, and prostitution is effectively marketed in the country's largest tabloid newspaper, *Ekstra Bladet,* and on web pages. Prostitution is being served to Danish men on a silver plate as a sexually legitimate choice, at the same time as all the political parties in the country agree on one thing: that prostitution is a social problem and therefore *not* an occupation. The state, nevertheless, levies taxes from the income of this social problem, and there is neither legislation against advertising prostitution nor any on the horizon. Of course, this is very useful for the sex industry and the many people who profit from the prostitution of others. However, it also expresses a very problematic clash of interests between the values of society and reality.

It has not been documented whether the number of johns has increased, or if the increase in prostitution has to do with the frequency with which men buy sex. Even so, the growth in the number of

---

[99] *Prostitution i Danmark,* Rasmussen, Servicestyrelsen, 2007, p. 83: http://www.servicestyrelsen.dk/udgivelser/udsatte/prostitution/prostitution-i-danmark
[100] The figures are based on C. Lautrup's report: *Det skal ikke bare være en krop mod krop-oplevelse,* VFC Socialt Udsatte, 2005.

prostitutes over the last 20 years indicates that there may be an increase in men's consumption of prostitution.

The Resistance

The Danish feminist movement has been actively engaged in the fight against trafficking on many levels but has not, until recently, presented a united front on the prostitution issue. I personally hesitated before I got involved, as I was fully aware that my involvement would not win me any popularity contests after the Danish sex buyer was caught red-handed with his trousers down around his shoes. From my international work, I also knew that the prostitution agenda provokes violent criticism from many quarters. Becoming engaged in the fight against prostitution is therefore an uphill struggle, one that is lonely and dirty. Your character is blackened and they try to silence you; you are threatened and made to look ridiculous. You are up against enormous and powerful financial forces with a crucial stake in making you shut up and maintaining the status quo in the area. The fight is also sad in itself, because you come into contact with people who have had their lives destroyed in prostitution, and you can no longer ignore the effects of prostitution in society. Therefore, the joint effort of fighting the devastation of the sex industry is crucial, since it is the support from this co-operation that gives us the energy to continue the fight, even though it would be much easier to give up.

Since 14% of Danish men have bought sex once or multiple times in their lives, it is only natural to ask the remaining 86% who have not bought sex what their views are on the matter. The fight against prostitution and trafficking should, in reality, be fronted by men. Limiting the extent of prostitution and trafficking of human beings can only succeed if the demand for prostitution is limited, which again means that men's right to buy sex should be removed. It is therefore first and foremost men who ought to have the ability to create a lasting change in the conduct of other men. Compared to women, men have more power when it comes to politics and wealth, and it is men who buy sex that finance prostitution with their money. Thus, prostitution is a gendered problem.

When the feminist movement rose up against prostitution and de-manded the prohibition of buying sex, it was long overdue. We wanted to do it in collaboration with men, to make them start discussing the buying of sex with each other. We wanted to create a change, which meant that men would become conscious of sex and take responsibility for their actions. We wanted them to take a stand and say no to prostitu-tion. We wanted to do away with the narrow conception of sexuality ex-pressed through one of the overlooked myths of prostitution—namely, that male sexuality is so strong that men turn to rape if there is no ac-cess to prostitution. In other words, men have no sexual self-control. But the question then became: Would the Danish feminist movement make a demand for a prohibition of the buying of sex in Denmark? And: would the feminist movement join a broad coalition to regenerate an effective 8th of March (International Women's Day) Movement to act as a platform for this demand? The answer was yes.

In the fall of 2007, we called a meeting with the intention of joint-ly revitalising a strong 8th of March movement that would demand a prohibition against the buying of sex. Twenty-three women's or-ganisations, youth organisations, political parties, and social institu-tions joined ranks and formed the network called the 8th of March Initiative (8. marts-initiativet—www.8marts.dk). At the time of this writing, three years later, we are still going strong and have grown to 29 organisations. That dark autumn night three years ago, we hit a momentum, as they call it in marketing language. Everyone had had enough of the expanding sex industry, of all the trafficking, the slavery, and the sexualised exploitation of women. Everyone had had enough of the narrow definition of human sexuality and the myth of prostitution as both essential for the sexual survival of men and free choice for women.

The fight to deprive men, as a gender, of the privilege of buying sex is the most important feminist issue at the moment, as it is all about giving women control over their own bodies and sexuality. If we do not win this fight, the feminist backlash in Denmark will continue. And it has already lasted too long.

The Work of the 8th of March Initiative

The general ideas behind the political work of the 8th of March Initiative have been:

- that prostitution should be seen as sexualised violence against human beings
- that prostitution is a gendered problem
- that prostitution quite preposterously categorises all men as brutes who cannot control their own sexuality—an allegation that we simply do not believe
- that patriarchal structures and mechanisms are the reason for prostitution and that these structures limit both sexes
- that the fight to prohibit the buying of sex can be won if it is well organised
- that the fight against prostitution ought to be fought jointly by both sexes
- that a joint slogan together with a joint demand to "Ban the buying of sex now!" across political and gender differences make us strong

The 8th of March Initiative strives to promote public resistance to the sexual exploitation of human beings in prostitution. The exploitation in prostitution is so gross that it is necessary to set aside differences in political views and ideological hobbyhorses. The issue is simply too serious for disagreement, which is why the 8th of March Initiative is a broad movement consisting of young and old people, of left- and right-wingers, and of women and men.

With our first major demonstration in 2008, we wanted to provide an opportunity for a broad discussion of values as a structural base: What kind of society do we want to live in? Do we want more or less prostitution? Why do men not take responsibility as a gender/group for their sexuality? How can we achieve emancipation for all women as long as our sex can be sold? Prostitution is sexualised violence and does not fit into the conception of the welfare state as a socially responsible society that attends to the most marginalised groups within.

By prohibiting the buying of sex, pimps and traffickers will come under strong pressure. It will become far more difficult to open brothels and other prostitution establishments because of the extended control and focus from the authorities. The threat of punitive measures and disclosure will make many johns change their conduct and will force them to stop buying sex. Sweden introduced a prohibition against the buying of sex in 1999 and today has one of the smallest prostitution markets in Europe. It is a reality that many try to hide, ignore, or explain away. But who believes that Swedish men have less desire than other men, and that this is the reason? It is hard to get around the fact that an ongoing Swedish public debate about (and a definition of) prostitution as violence against women, and caused by women's subordinate position, *in combination with* a law against the buying of sex, as well as strong enforcement thereof by the police, are essential reasons for the successful reduction of prostitution in Sweden.

In an English survey from 2009, out of 103 London johns questioned, two-thirds of them said that if they were given a sentence for buying sex, it would prevent them from doing it.[101] If we actually want to reduce the extent of prostitution and trafficking in human beings, society ought not to shrink from taking punitive measures toward conduct that has such great human and social costs as prostitution and trafficking.

UN conventions and policy statements command the Danish state to reduce the number of men who buy sex, but despite information campaigns, the number of sex buyers has not decreased. Documentaries, books, media features, discussions, and the like have not limited the number of men who buy sex. Johns will not let themselves be limited in the absence of legislation.

The Many Faces of the Resistance

The 8th of March Initiative has made use of a broad spectrum of work methods. We have lobbied and entered into alliances with other organisations, we have made networks and held seminars, we have engaged in pro-active as well as re-active media work, we have had our own booths

---

[101] See the report "Men who buy sex. Who they buy and what they know," Eaves, 2009, http://www.eaves4women.co.uk/Documents/Recent_Reports/

on different occasions (women's fairs, Labour Day, etc.) and held count-less meetings, meetings, meetings. We have participated in conferences and arranged demonstrations. In other words, we have been quite busy.

On 8th of March, 2008, 1,700 people walked through Copenhagen in the first big demonstration against prostitution and trafficking under the slogan "Ban the buying of sexual services now!"[102] At the same time, the Danish Women's Society (*Dansk Kvindesamfund*), an organisation of which I am a member, created an Internet campaign called "Take a Stand, Man!" that was launched on March 1, 2008.[103] With the campaign, we hoped to get answers from some of the 86% of men who do *not* buy sex, and to hear their thoughts on men, prostitution, and the buying of sex. Together with a feminist colleague, Mette Poulsen, who is also a member of Danish Women's Society, I sat down and wrote to hundreds of known and unknown men, and asked them to take a stand and support a prohibition against the buying of sex. They were then to send a photo and write down the reasons for their support. They were also asked to answer these three questions:

- Why is it important that men take a stand against the buying of sex?
- Why is it necessary to prohibit the buying of sex by law?
- What is the most important reason to criminalise the johns?

More than 120 men joined the campaign, among them some of the country's most influential media people: politicians from the Danish Social Democrats (*Socialdemokraterne*), the Socialist People's Party (*Socialistisk Folkeparti*), the Red-Green Alliance (*Enhedslisten*), the Danish Social Liberal Party (*De Radikale),* athletes, musicians, artists, and so on. There were also men from the trade unions, among them the chairman of 3F, the chairman of FOA (Trade and Labour), and the chairman of LO (the Danish Confederation of Trade Unions).[104] Nobody

---

[102] See the homepage of the March 8th Initiative: www.8marts.dk

[103] www.tagstillingmand.dk

[104] 3F stands for the United Federation of Danish Workers and organises skilled and un-skilled workers, primarily in the private sector. FOA stands for Trade and Labour and or-ganises primarily members in the public sector. LO stands for the Danish Confederation of Trade Unions, the largest national trade union confederation in Denmark.

had believed that so many men would have the courage to show their faces and give their whole-hearted support to the fight for limiting prostitution in Denmark. We were very happy and surprised, and so was Denmark. Both the media, which had run amok, and the (ir)responsibility of the invisible john were brought up for discussion as our political opponents came out of their closets.

Five days after the launch of the Internet campaign "Take a Stand, Man!" the Sexworkers' Interest Group (*Sexarbejdernes Interesseorganisation*, or SIO) was established, and they immediately became the darlings of the media. Prostitutes who claimed that they liked being prostitutes came forward, and the media made a fortune, as this fitted perfectly into the widely accepted myth of prostitution as free choice. In those days, the organisation Sexual Politic Forum (*Seksualpolitisk Forum*), the crusaders of Danish open-mindedness, wore several keyboards out by zealously writing and blogging to tell the Danes that the 8th of March Initiative was terribly wrong, and that prostitution was an expression of sexual open-mindedness. The 8th of March Initiative was insulted in the most distinguished manner and got the usual hate mail, and we were very, very proud.

The 120 men who joined the Internet campaign were also subjected to ridicule. They were met with the same reasoning that is being used against women who rebel: they were made to look silly, or they were ignored. Not a single television interview was conducted with any of the participants who had taken a stand in support of the criminalisation of johns. Despite the fact that SIO had done an aggressive mailing to a great number of the participants to tell them that they were completely mistaken in their views on prostitution, not one of the 120 men withdrew from the campaign.

The advocates for the legalisation of prostitution and licensed brothels in Denmark, Sexual Politic Forum and SIO, have been deeply influenced by the experiences of countries with legalised sex industries such as New Zealand, Germany, and The Netherlands. The Danish pro-prostitution lobby paints an idyllic picture of the conditions in the sex industry in these countries. However, they seem to overlook the fact that the authorities in Germany and The Netherlands have started to recognise publicly that legalising prostitution has not worked out the way it was intended to.[105] The experience of these countries shows that extending the rights of prostitutes by making it legal to exploit the prostitution of others and redefining pimps as businessmen has not made conditions better for prostitutes. Instead it has given the sex industry a boost and has engineered a tremendous growth in the trafficking of human beings.[106]

Prostitution is about a systemic sexual oppression of women, but the rejection of this truth has come from the most unexpected places. One of the most persistent opponents of the 8th of March Initiative turned out to be the then-deputy director of the Danish Institute for Human Rights. She fought in the media and lobbied politically in order to introduce a smiley arrangement in Danish brothels by which johns could see on the door that here you would get voluntary, clean, and VAT-registered (taxable) prostitution. She actually believed that the UN's CEDAW convention grants women the right to prostitute themselves, and we had to realise that even though people may be experts and have law degrees in human rights, they may still read UN conventions just as the devil quotes scripture to his purpose.[107] In truth, this was a reinterpretation of the intention behind Article 6 in the CEDAW convention, which orders states to limit trafficking in women and the exploitation of women's prostitution on the grounds that prostitution is regarded as sexual exploitation and not as a free choice or as work.

Other Danish opponents of the criminalisation of johns can be found among independent groups on the extreme left, in queer circles, and in liberal groups such as the youth organisations of the political parties Left, Liberal Party of Denmark (*Venstre*), and the Danish Social Liberal Party (*Det Radikale Venstre*).[108] The Women's House in Copenhagen is divided on the issue; the Women's Camp Femø Group is a member of the 8th of March Initiative; and other groups in the house support the

---

[105] See, for instance, the homepage of the German Ministry of Justice, http://www.bmj.bund.de and the German Ministry of the Families, http://www.bmfsfj.de

[106] See "Trafficking in Human Beings—Sixth Report of the Dutch National Rapporteur," 2008.

[107] See www.berlingske.dk/danmark/prostitution-som-en-rettighed-kvinder

[108] Venstre is currently in power, and its leader is the Prime Minister Lars Løkke Rasmussen.

individualistic discourse about prostitution as a free choice that eman-
cipates women.[109] Moreover, some of our opponents can be found in
academic circles, especially among social scientists, as well as among
some politicians, particularly on the right. There are also various blog-
gers who are busy on the Internet stating their opinions of and against
us, but being cowards when it comes to making themselves known by
face and name. Thus, on the prostitution issue, the extreme left wing
shares political aims with large parts of the right wing, because they
reduce prostitution to a question of achieving rights for employers and
employees. They also promote prostitution as a free and emancipating
choice and believe that it should be considered an ordinary trade in
which the market forces should be given free rein by legalising pimps
and licensing brothels.

The Media Machine
In the wake of the 8th of March Initiative's demand for a law against
the buying of sex in 2008, and the Danish Women's Society's campaign
www.tagstillingmand.dk, the Danish newspapers overflowed with articles about the disaster that would befall Denmark if it became illegal to
buy sex. Some media tried to spin the agenda in another direction and
away from the responsibility of men who buy sex. Regarding the media,
the most difficult challenge has been—and still is—the many unsubstan-
tiated assertions about, for example, the effect of introducing a law that
limits the demand for prostitution. These untruths stand unchallenged
in spoken as well as print media, because journalists fail to research the
subject thoroughly. The myths of prostitution and the romantic conception of it are still rife, and the public is heavily misinformed.

It did not surprise us that the anti-feminist newspaper *Ekstra Bladet*
carried on a smear campaign against us when we posed our demand
to criminalise the johns. Any other reaction would have disappointed
us. After all, the existence of *Ekstra Bladet* depends on its 40–60 million Danish kroner in yearly profit from prostitution ads. It was more

---

[109] The Women's House (Kvindehuset in Danish) in Copenhagen was established in 1971
and now houses different women's groups, such as the Femø Group, which arranged the
first women's camps on the island of Femø, and the Sexworkers' Interest Group (SIO).

problematic, however, that the newspaper *Information* blackened the characters of feminists and found them unworthy as debaters—especially because it has been the left wing that has traditionally fought for social justice and expressed solidarity with oppressed groups in society. In the prostitution debate, *Information*, the most popular newspaper on the left, has been dominated by individualistic and liberalistic discourse: prostitution is a free choice and empowers women, and it should be legal to profit from the prostitution of others. The perspective of power and gender has not been dealt with in the paper; instead, it nourishes the image of the satisfied prostitute who acts out her sexuality through prostitution. The paper has also ignored the serious structural imbalances underlying the sex industry—not to mention the serious level of crime that is connected with the sex industry and the strong financial interests that are at stake, since it is extremely profitable to sell other people in prostitution. *Information*'s own reasoning has been built on pseudo-scientific analyses and a violent pushback against the opponents of prostitution. Many articles have promoted the legalisation model that New Zealand has introduced. The newspaper has chosen not to be critical toward the reports from New Zealand about legalisation, and it has left out important areas such as trafficking in women and the prostitution of minors. The study can also be criticised in terms of the research, as it offers alarming figures on violence and other forms of exploitation of prostitutes. Apart from that, the authorities in New Zealand hardly keep in check the sex industry in that country.[110]

The Sexworkers' Interest Group (SIO) has quickly become the primary source for the media when they need a comment from a prostitute. SIO had 181 members as of 2011,[111] not all of whom have experience in prostitution but profit from the sex industry in other ways. It is therefore a serious problem that SIO has become the mouthpiece for all prostitutes, because it means that the experiences of prostitutes who want to stop and former prostitutes who now suffer from psycho

---

[110] See Prostitution Law Review Committee, Ministry of Justice, 2008: www.justice.govt.nz/policy-and-consultation/legislation/prostitution-law-review-committee
[111] See *Årsberetning 2010* (Annual report 2010), http://s-i-o.dk/tekst/aarsberetning-2010.pdf

logical damage are not being heard in the public debate. To change this situation, we started to find women who are in favour of criminalising the johns and who have experience in prostitution in order to include them in the discussion, though the costs of participating are very high. The few courageous women with experience in prostitution, who struggle with the hurtful consequences of it and still rebel against the normalisation and romaticisation of prostitution in the public debate, pay a very, very high price. They are being ridiculed, threatened, and harassed, and their personal and hard-earned experience that corroborates the fact that prostitution has destroyed some of their survival potential are being ignored.

These courageous few have hundreds and hundreds of voices whispering behind them—voices silently thanking them for speaking up. They not only speak on behalf of women who have left prostitution and who have been damaged. They speak on behalf of all women, including those of us who have not been prostitutes, because it is our sisters all over the world who primarily end up in prostitution because they happen to be born without the same opportunities as us.

Changes in the Political Landscape
During the first year of the 8th of March Initiative, the prostitution debate in Denmark shifted from a primary focus on fighting trafficking to the discussion for and against the prohibition of buying sex, and about the experiences of Norway and Sweden. Even so, the pro-prostitution discourse garnered much coverage in the media because it was considered to be sexier. Much was written about—and still is written about—prostitution as a free choice and as an ordinary job that lacks only labour rights. The pro-prostitution lobby—consisting of SIO, the Sexual Politic Forum, and the newspaper *Information* as its standard-bearer, led an aggressive campaign in the media about legalisation in New Zealand. The lobby succeeded in describing that step as a huge success, because no journalists took the trouble to research it to determine if it was really true. If they had done their work properly, they would have found that the content as well as the research methods being used in the report from New Zealand are highly questionable.

In 2009, the 8th of March Initiative succeeded in intensifying the political pressure on the pro-prostitution lobby and gave hope to the citizens of Copenhagen that it was possible to fight the sex industry. More than 1,000 people demonstrated on 8th of March in the pouring rain and walked through Copenhagen's brothel centre, Istedgade, again with the joint slogan "Ban the buying of sex now!" A speech by the party leader of the Socialist People's Party, Villy Søvndal, who is currently one of the most popular politicians in Denmark, kicked off the demonstration, an event that clearly showed our strength.

For a long time, the Socialist People's Party and the Red-Green Alliance were the only political parties that supported a prohibition of the buying of sex. However, in September 2009, a big political breakthrough took place. The Danish Social Democrats debated the criminalisation issue at their annual party conference and decided to work on a party-political level toward a prohibition of the buying of sex. Their youth organisation is a member of the 8th of March Initiative and had worked hard through the years to make it happen. The 8th of March Initiative also played a crucial role in the year prior to the conference. The decision of the Danish Social Democrats was extremely encouraging to the many activists that have worked hard to maintain the steam in the prostitution pressure-cooker. The resistance to the right to buying sex is now shifting to the centre of Danish politics.

In most of the non-Socialist and Liberal parties, there is massive resistance to criminalisation of johns among the party leadership. However, in the Liberal Party there are members who are rooted in the Grundtvigian way of thinking, as well as in civic decency, that support our agenda. According to an opinion poll from September 2009, 29% of the voters of the Liberal Party supported the demand for a prohibition of the buying of sex.[112] A single politician, Marion Pedersen, who represents the Liberal Party in the Danish Parliament, has bravely supported this strategy from the beginning of the 8th of March Initiative, even though her party has decided not to take a stand on the question.[113] It is

---

[112] See Jyllands Postens's web page: http://jp.dk/indland/indland_politik/article1822697.ece
[113] See the Internet campaign "Tag stilling, mand!" at: www.tagstillingmand.dk/presse/marion_pedersen_tale.shtml

hard to believe that there are no members of the Conservative People's Party who want to fight against the demand for prostitution and trafficking, even though their party leadership is against it and/or has kept silent about it.

The Danish Social-Liberal Party has also discussed the criminalisation issue at the last party conference, and has, for the time being, decided to support a criminalisation of men who buy sex from prostitutes who "have entered involuntarily into the trade."[114] This is the model that has been used in Finland, for instance, and the model that the man on the street knows as the "Buy Danish Model." The model is completely ineffective, but we regard the party's decision as a temporary political compromise and a step in the right direction.

The Trends in the Danish Debate on Prostitution

The Danish debate on prostitution has tended to focus on the many myths of prostitution—prostitution is a free choice, prostitution is a way of combating rape, prostitution is necessary for handicapped persons, or prostitution is inevitable. The 8th of March Initiative does not recognise that the premise upon which the Danish prostitution policy rests is the idea of free choice. Even people in prostitution who believe that prostitution is the right choice for them are exposed to considerable risk of lasting damage. It is impossible to tell beforehand whether you will be damaged or not. The very few Danish women who have escaped prostitution and dared to come forward with their experiences and spoken hopefully of a prohibition against the buying of sex, were themselves active ambassadors for the myth of free choice when they were still in prostitution. However, the damage they have suffered because of prostitution, which they have to live with the rest of their lives, has made them change their minds. They now fight for society to reduce the demand for prostitution.

Just as in the other Nordic countries, the Danish prostitution devotees have argued that a prohibition on purchasing will drive prostitution underground, and, as a result, the conditions for prostitutes will

---

[114] See the party's web page: http://radikale.dk/public/upload/Filer/RVResolutioner LM2009.pdf

worsen. This argument implies that we know what is going on in the sex industry today, but the truth is that prostitution in Denmark takes place out of reach of the authorities. There is no control of what actually takes place in the Danish brothels, and no one knows what the large group of escort prostitutes is being exposed to. Sex is, to a large extent, sold via the Internet and mobile phones, so the number of women involved in prostitution is always uncertain. What we do know is that these inexact numbers are enormous, since the authorities hardly ever carry out any inspections in the area. Since prostitution is *trading* in sex, it requires that the men who buy sex are able to find the goods in order to establish a contact between the buyer and the seller. To monitor and find these contacts is only a question of priorities. Society must allocate the needed resources to it—especially on the part of the police force.

One of the important arguments on the left against the criminalisation of men who buy sex has been that meting out a sentence is not a productive response to a social problem. This is an anti-feminist point of view. First, we are not talking about increasing a pre-existing sentence; rather, we want society to recognise that prostitution is a serious social problem involving sexualised violence, and that making use of prostitution should therefore be treated as a crime. Second, a constitutional state comes to the rescue of women, and feminists ought to support sentences for assault, murder, and violence. Nobody disagrees that rape and murder must be prohibited. Exposing another person to the risk of destroying his or her life by prostitution must also be prohibited. I am in favour of leniency in sentencing, but society has had difficulties in recognising that violence against women should be a criminal offence to begin with. This is also the reason why feminists have fought long and hard to increase sentences for rape. Sanction in itself is not an evil of society—especially not for women.

The trench warfare between the advocates for and the opponents of the buying of sex has lasted for almost three years now. The actions and culpability of the men who buy sex have gradually become more and more visible. Today, no one in Denmark discusses the subject of prostitution without also discussing whether he or she is for or against criminalising the johns. The damaging effects of a life in prostitution, along with the growth in the trafficking of women and the Danish sex industry, has also become a natural part of the debate.

The 8th of March Initiative has been told off countless times—a certain sign of success! To be on the receiving end of opposition, harassment, and abusive language is a badge of nobility, because it means that we are being heard and that we are influential.

A New Danish Model?

Neither Sweden nor Norway has accompanied the introduction of a law against the buying of sex with sufficient social initiatives. This mistake must not be repeated in Denmark, and the 8th of March Initiative has therefore worked from the beginning toward a Danish model. This model will rest on two pillars: one that deals with the legislative side of the matter and reduces the demand by making it illegal to buy sex, and one that deals with social initiatives, including nationwide exit programs that will get people out of prostitution by offering a wide range of options of a legal, psychological, health, and labour market-oriented nature. The prostitutes who continue in prostitution after the introduction of a prohibition against the buying of sex do not commit a crime and may therefore contact the authorities for advice and help without being exposed to reprisals of a financial nature. Among other things, it will be necessary to find a solution to the problem that many women in prostitution receive public benefits at the same time that they have an income from prostitution.

The English survey of men who buy sex shows that more than 70% of the 103 men often felt guilty or shameful about the fact that they had bought sex.[115] This, however, did not make them stop buying sex; it merely made them keep it a secret. This ambivalence has good potential for making them change their conduct, and it ought to be made use of. A prohibition on the buying of sex should be supplemented by an efficient offer for guidance to the men who want to stop buying sex but who need support in order to make their wish come true. Another important

---

[115] See the report "Men who buy sex: Who they buy and what they know," Eaves, 2009, www.eaves4women.co.uk

area that must be focused on is the implementation of the law, because it is crucial to its success that the police force and the judicial system get training in making use of the law in practice and combining it with already-existing legislation in the prostitution area. Furthermore, comparative studies should be carried out in order to analyse the prostitution market before the introduction of a prohibition, and then again 5 and 10 years later. In addition to this, the authorities should make a massive preventive effort among the young a priority. The conditions faced by victims of human trafficking for prostitution are an extremely complicated area that should be a constant focus. Denmark should take its ratification of the UN's Palermo Protocols seriously and make sure that people who have been victims of trafficking for prostitution can achieve a permanent residence permit in Denmark. For the time being, the legal status of these people, as well as their prospects for the future, are more or less non-existent, which again means that they are often forced to continue as prostitutes.

The Attainable Utopia
A prohibition of the buying of sex will tilt the balance of power among all citizens in a society and will set a completely new agenda for the way society looks at the sexes in the future. This will force us to find new ways to understand ourselves as members of a gender and as sexual beings, and it will support women in making more demands for a life in which they are free individuals with self-determination over their own bodies and sexuality. This will force society to change its reified view on women especially, and will open new paths for the formation of identities in generations to come. It will force men to relate to themselves as a group, as a sex, and as men in possession of power—and it will make them contemplate how to use, and especially how *not* to use, their power.

Much too often the emancipation of women is said to be an important issue, whereas in practice it is often subordinated to the *essential* political questions—another way of saying that women's emancipation is not that important after all. Moreover, it is often said that we are emancipated and have reached our goal, so stop complaining! The emancipation of women and the equal opportunities that society boasts of on special occasions are merely empty phrases as long as society accepts that so many people must risk having their lives destroyed in the sex industry, the majority of whom are women, and as long as we have sex slavery in Denmark.

The core issue in the emancipation of women is to change the way society perceives women, that is, to see women as whole human beings and not to reduce them to sexualised body parts. This will have a bearing on all other feminist projects of emancipation: the possibility of achieving equal pay, the possibility of breaking the gender divide of the labour market, the possibility of making men use their paternity leave, and so on. The demand for a prohibition of the buying of sex is therefore incendiary, as it will remove the structural barriers of society and touch on the most fundamental power imbalance between women and men.

Prostitution and the Commercial Value of Youth

Rachel Moran

People who argue that prostitution would be free of coercion, trafficking, the exploitation of minors—and everything else that prevents it from being some kind of all-above-board, consenting-adults-only autonomy party—are people who ignore one vital aspect of prostitution's reality. It is the commercial value of youth.

Just as in some actual industries such as modelling or professional dance, youth is a highly prized attribute. Unlike modelling or dance, though, youth in prostitution is prized far above beauty and the fluidity of movement. In order to be the most highly in demand in prostitution, you don't need to be the prettiest flower in the field; you just need to be among the youngest. And what you can or cannot do with your body is irrelevant. It just matters that it hasn't been on the planet for very long.

One of the most common questions that comes through on any brothel's phone line is "What age is the youngest girl you have?" I cannot count the times I have been asked that question, and I defy anybody who has answered a brothel's phone to tell the blatant lie that it is not the commonest question they've been asked, too.

The commercial value of youth is so profoundly built into prostitution that women routinely lie about their age in order to generate more business. The clients know this, of course, and even as women are shaving a few years off, clients are adding a few on. "I'm twenty-six—I'll tell him I'm twenty-three" / "She's twenty-three?—That means she's twenty-six."

Nobody's fooling anybody here, and the only thing the whole pathetic charade is any good for is the revealing nature of what's going on behind the pretence. What it reveals, of course, is that men who buy bodies for sex usually want to buy the youngest body they can find.

Last year it was reported to the BBC that prostitutes as young as 13 were working the streets in Swindon, in the English county of Wiltshire. "Come here at the weekend and you'll get 13-year-old girls to 19-year-old girls out here," one prostitute told reporters.

When I read reports like these I just sigh. It tires me to pre-empt the shock people will express. It tires me to imagine that shock, whether it is genuine or not, because if it is genuine, then that proves we have a long way to go in educating people about the reality of prostitution, and if it is not, well then, here is yet more in a tsunami of evidence that there are those who do not want the reality of prostitution understood.

Whenever any evidence of teenage prostitution is revealed, the pro-prostitution lobby move immediately to put forth the preposterous assertion that this town is somehow different or unique. The attitude is always either "thirteen-year-olds, good Lord, who ever heard of such a thing?"—or "thirteen-year-olds, good Lord, we could clear up this situation if we legalised prostitution!"—as if somehow the demand for adolescent bodies would vanish if only we'd make the sale of adult bodies okay!

Usually, however, they will simply deny that adolescent prostitution is widespread, or that adolescents are much in demand in the first place.

"How do we know this is true?" will come the query from the pro-prostitution lobby. It is not a query in the genuine sense of the word. A real query seeks an answer. This query seeks to obscure the same answer it purports to be seeking.

This will seem strange and confusing to some people. It is neither strange nor confusing to me; I've been exposed to the tactics of the pro-prostitution lobby for too long to be surprised or confused by these sorts of seemingly tangled and nonsensical tactics. What people need to understand is that they are not nonsensical. These are obscurist policies that are purposeful and predictable, and when you understand their purpose, you will have no problem predicting them, too.

Their purpose is consistent: it is to deny and refute the sick and twisted nature of what actually goes on in prostitution. The truth they don't want you to know is that men who pay for sex will most often opt to pay for a 15-year-old over a 17-year-old, a 17-year-old over a 19-year-old, a 19-year-old over a 21-year-old, and so on and so forth.

Now, let me be very clear about this—I will be called a liar for having asserted the above. It will be said that I am trying to demonise johns, that I am telling lies about their preferences and proclivities. I wish I were. In my first year in prostitution, when I was 15 years old, I was used by countless hundreds of men; I truly couldn't say how many. I saw up to ten men a day, so you may do the math for yourself (the thoughts of doing that calculation disturbs me). As I stated in my Examiner article back in February, men were so obviously aroused by my youth it made them climax very quickly, so I soon learned to tell them how old I was in order to shorten the whole ordeal. I made it a policy; it was one of the first things I said when I got into the car—not that I needed to bring up the subject because it was usually one of the first questions asked of me.

Of all those hundreds of men, one man, just ONE, turned his van around and brought me back to where he'd found me.

So yes, those who advocate for legalised or decriminalised prostitution will do their damnedest to obscure the truth about the high commercial value placed on young bodies in prostitution, all the while squawking, "Where's the evidence? Where's the evidence?'—like some kind of belligerent and demented parrot with all the repetitiveness and severe comprehension issues you'd expect. All beak and no brains, in other words.

This is to be expected. Of course the pro-prostitution lobby don't want you to know that girls who are post-puberty by only a year or two are routinely lusted after, sought out, highly prized, and then abused for enough years 'til they've lost much of their commercial value. If that were widely known, it would do a great deal of damage to the autonomous, sexually liberated, empowerment fantasy depiction they are consistently trying to peddle.

As for "Where's the evidence?"—I don't need to ask that question. When I was a 15-year-old prostitute I was far more in demand than I ever was as a 22-year-old, even though at 22 I was slim, pretty, and an extremely youthful woman. But therein lies the problem. I was a woman.

There is huge emphasis placed on the commercial value of youth in prostitution. "The evidence" is in every brothel and red-light zone in the land, and I know that because I lived the evidence.

I know it because I was the evidence.

The Crusade of the Pro-Prostitution Lobby

Ane Stø and Asta Håland

The OECD estimates that every year at least 500,000 persons are sold into prostitution in Europe. At the moment, the discussion in many countries centres on strategies for fighting violence against women, prostitution, and organised crime, especially since prostitution was legalised and declared to be common "sex work" around the turn of the millennium. This legalisation took place in Austria and Greece in 1998, in The Netherlands in 2000, and in Germany in 2002. In Europe, the liberalistic model—in which women from less developed countries are imported to a country alongside other goods—has been promoted by The Netherlands, Denmark, and Germany.

But legalisation as a means to control and regulate the sex industry has not had its intended result. Instead, a large illegal industry, hiding behind the legal brothels, has been created. To define prostitution as an occupation like any other does not help secure the rights of prostitutes, but rather bolsters the income of procurers and human traffickers. Now the Nordic model—criminalising the act of buying, but not selling, sexual services—is being discussed in France, Albania, Finland, Scotland, and Ireland. Even in liberal Denmark, strong forces are working toward following the example of Sweden, Norway, and Iceland in their legislation, as trust in the German/Dutch model is eroding. The empirical evidence is clear: a ban on buying sexual services does have its intended results.

The Fall of Legalisation

According to the German Health Department there were close to 400,000 prostitutes in Germany in 2012. Arnold Plickert, deputy chairman of the German Police Association, tells RP online that "the politicians have shot themselves in the foot by implementing this law. Even though it was well intended, it has only strengthened the criminals."[116] According to police authorities, prostitution is an enormous market, its yearly turnover about 14.5 billion. Before brothels and procuring prostitutes were made legal, supporters of legalisation claimed the prostitutes' lives would improve through workers' rights, unions, and access to health insurance. But none of these promises has come true. Both before and after legalisation, more than 80% of the women working in the brothels were Eastern European or Asian, most of them illegal immigrants.

Der Spiegel published a long article in May 2013 describing how legalisation has resulted in fewer rights and lower rewards for prostitutes in Germany.[117] Munich Police Chief Wilhelm Schmidbauer tells about an explosive increase in trafficking from Romania and Bulgaria. In 2006, five years after legalisation was implemented, the German ministry of family politics evaluated the law. According to Der Spiegel, the report concluded that the law had led to no noticeable improvement for the prostitutes. Nor was there any evidence that deregulation had led to any reduction in crime. German police officers complain that they are no longer given permission to investigate brothels. Germany has become a "centre for sexual abuse of young women from Eastern Europe, and a playground for organised criminals from all over the world," a retired police officer tells Der Spiegel.

The Netherlands legalised prostitution in 2000 by repealing the ban against brothels and procuring. The reasoning behind the move was that, as prostitution is impossible to fight, the conditions for people in the prostitution business would improve if there were no legal sanctions. The goal of the legalisation policies was to gain control over the prostitution industry through municipal licensing in order to hinder

---

[116] http:/www.rp-online.de
[117] *Der Spiegel* 22/2013 (May 26, 2013).

forced prostitution, to protect minors from sexual abuse, to improve the circumstances for people working in prostitution, to weaken the link between prostitution and criminal environments, and to reduce the scope of trafficking.

In 2008 the Dutch police department conducted a survey which concluded that the legalisation policies had failed completely. The report estimated that 50–90% of the women in the legalised prostitution industry were "working involuntarily," that one way or another their labor was forced. The Daalder report from 2007[118] examined the circumstances in prostitution in 2006 vis-à-vis government goals and concluded that the legalisation policies had been a fiasco. The goal to regulate "voluntary" prostitution had not been achieved, and the researchers found that most of the sex industry was still operating illegally. Legalisation has made prostitution more common and acceptable, while the profit for the facilitators increases when they can avoid taxes, labour inspections, and health controls.

After 13 years of full legalisation, Dutch authorities have no idea of the number of minors in prostitution. Police controls have decreased the presence of minors in the legal part of the industry, but the number of minors working in the illegal part of the prostitution industry is unknown.[119] The primary goal of legalisation was to improve working conditions for the prostitutes, but the reports are devastating on this point. After six years of legalisation, the emotional well being of the prostitutes was significantly lower than before, and the use of sedatives had increased. Many sought help in leaving the prostitution industry, but only 6% of municipalities offer such help.

The problems that The Netherlands and Germany are facing in their struggle to regulate the aggressive prostitution industry are never mentioned by those who wish to facilitate for prostitution. On the contrary, they are spreading lies about the Nordic model internationally, lies that we need to refute over and over again. Since the Swedish Sex Purchase Act was implemented in 1999, the pro-prostitution lobby has been spreading propaganda globally, claiming the law hasn't had its

---

[118] *Prostitution in The Netherlands since the lifting of the brothel ban*, A.L. Daalder (2007).
[119] *On legalised prostitution in The Netherlands*, Karin Werkman (2011).

intended effect. Since Norway and Iceland followed Sweden's lead in 2009, they have increased their efforts in this field. The Nordic model has become a very real threat to the international trafficking industry, an industry that each year brings in billions of Euros.

Unfortunately, the Nordic model not only faces resistance from the international pro-prostitution lobby. In September 2013, Norwegian political parties such as the Liberal Party (Venstre), the Conservative Party (Høyre), the right-wing, populist Progress Party (Fremskrittspartiet), and the Green Party (Miljøpartiet de grønne) made repealing the Sex Purchase Act part of their election campaign. As we write this, a majority of the seats in the Norwegian Parliament (Stortinget) are held by parties wishing to repeal a law we consider to be an excellent tool for reducing prostitution, trafficking, and other organised crime. And this is happening only five years after the law was implemented.

Iceland not only placed a ban on the purchase of sexual services in 2009; they also banned strip clubs. The Icelandic government at the time even looked into developing an Internet porn filter in Iceland when they had to leave the cabinet last year. With the new Icelandic government, the porn filter is not going to happen, and the feminist movement is still fighting for the police to use the law against the johns.

In 2011, the majority of the current government coalition in Denmark made criminalising the purchase of sexual services an election promise, but only a year later, the Social Democratic Party changed their position on this topic and put the blame on one of the smaller coalition parties. As we can see, the opponents of the Nordic model have had their share of victories over the last five years. Why, and how, are the cheerleaders of prostitution now gaining ground in the Nordic countries?

Evaluation of the Swedish Sex Purchase Act

Among the goals of the Swedish Sex Purchase Act that was implemented in 1999 were to prevent and reduce trafficking, to decrease the number of sex buyers, and to heighten public awareness. One also hoped the ban would help decrease men's sexualised violence against women and give the police an extra tool in their fight against trafficking and the prostitution industry.

In November 2010, the Swedish government's evaluation of the Sex Purchase Act was released: "Förbud mot köp av sexuell tjänst. En utvardering 1999–2008" ("Ban on Buying Sexual Services. A Survey, 1999–2008"). The evaluation was conducted by a committee led by Swedish Attorney General Anna Skarhed. The rest of the committee consisted of various experts on the field. The evaluation concerns the effects of the ban during its first nine years.

The main conclusion is that the law has had its intended effect and is an important tool in preventing and reducing prostitution. Today there is broad political unity on the importance and effects of the law. Police representatives state that Sweden has become a less attractive country for human traffickers as a result of the law. Street prostitution has been reduced by 50%, and there are fewer men buying sex than before. In 2013, 8% of Swedish men responded that they had bought sexual services; the figure for 1996 was 13%. This decline is attributed first and foremost to an increased awareness among Swedish men that buying sexual services is fundamentally wrong.

Despite the propaganda efforts of the pro-prostitution lobby internationally, there are no signs that violence against prostitutes has increased, or that prostitutes are experiencing worsened living conditions. Prostitutes are experiencing a situation in which they have more power over their own lives, as they are now able to report threatening customers to the police. The law has also made it easier for the women in prostitution to seek help to get out of their situation. It has not become more difficult for social services to establish contact with prostitutes, contrary to what many opponents of the law claim.

Interviews conducted among individuals who are still in prostitution and individuals who have gotten out of prostitution show that those who are still in prostitution are sceptical about the Sex Purchase Act and believe that their opinions go unheard. They also feel stigmatised as a group and need the protection of society. Those who have gotten out of prostitution have a consistently more positive opinion on the ban and believe it has given them the strength to leave prostitution, eliminating the blame for all the abuse they might have experienced.

As for the scope of prostitution, the evaluation states that, unlike in most other European countries, the prostitution trade in Sweden has stagnated, or even decreased slightly. Prostitution has been reduced by 50%, and there is no evidence pointing in the direction of it having moved to different arenas such as the indoor market. Further, there has been no increase in the number of brothels. All in all, there is nothing to suggest that the prostitution market has moved underground, and the police report having a good overview of the prostitution scene. The Sex Purchase Act gives the police better opportunities to take action against brothels, against human trafficking, and against the prostitution of minors.

The Swedish Debate

Even though 70% of the Swedish population supports the law, and the support is highest among the youngest segments of the population, it also has its enemies. Sweden has their own pro-prostitution lobby, represented by SANS (Sex Workers and Allies Network in Sweden), and the Rose Alliance (Sweden's national organisation for sex and erotic workers), who are part of the international pro-prostitution organisation Network of Sex Work Projects. Together with researchers such as Susanne Dodillet and pundits such as Petra Östergren, they energetically claim that sex work is like any other occupation. This position is also held by several right-wing politicians, as well as the think tank Timbro and the postmodern, left-wing journal Arena. The youth organisations associated with the Centre Party (Centerpartiet) and the liberal People's Party (Folkpartiet) have also embraced the idea that prostitution is really just another exciting occupation.

Östergren and Dodillet are very active in the Nordic prostitution debate and are working with pro-prostitution activists all over Europe to hinder the spread of the Nordic model. The Swedish writer Kajsa Ekis Ekman writes about how Petra Östergren's book Pornography, Whores and Feminists[120] pits "whores" and "feminists" against each other— the "whore" as the active subject, and the feminist as the puritanical

---

[120] *Porr, horor och feminister*, Östergren (2006).

oppressor.[121] Östergren interviewed 13 women in her book, all of whom claim to "love the role of the whore," have chosen to get into prostitution to avoid "dependency on men," "are breaking with the old female (gender) role," take "command over men," and have "a well-developed power analysis," according to Östergren. She claims that feminists, on the other hand, only want to protect and punish, and the resistance against the sex industry is only "about censorship and control."

According to this perspective, the prostitute is not a victim—she is a strong person who knows what she wants. This view of prostitution builds the foundation for Susanne Dodillet's 2009 PhD thesis in the History of Ideas, Är sex arbete? (Is Sex Work?). Dodillet believes that "the ban on buying sexual services gives sex sellers the role of passive victims, without the ability to make independent choices." Dodillet quotes Kirsten Frigstad, Norwegian PION's leading spokesperson, who says: "Most prostitutes are strong women who have taken responsibility for their situation, and they don't want to be described this way, for they are not victims in a traditional sense." Dodillet's claim is that in Sweden, unlike in Germany, "it is not the prostitutes themselves who have described their role," but politicians and social workers who have seen the prostitutes as "more or less helpless."

Östergren and Dodillet collaborated on the article "The Swedish Sex Purchase Act: Claimed Success and Documented Effects," which they have presented at several international conferences on prostitution. They dismiss existing research on the causes and effects of prostitution and instead continue their drama of good against evil. On one side they place "those women who have sexual relations with many men, and who sell their bodies for money," and on the other side they place "radical feminists and politicians."[122] They conclude that the law "has to do with a desire to create and uphold a national identity of being the moral consciousness in the world; with notions of "good" and "bad" sexuality; with the whore stigma; with creating new forms of sexual deviancy; with a communitarian, rather than liberal, political culture;

---

[121] *Varat och varan: prostitution, surrogatmödraskap och den delade människan*, Kajsa Ekis Ekman (2008).
[122] *Varat och varan*, Ekman (2008).

and perhaps above all, a stereotypical and uninformed understanding of prostitution."[123] In other words, they are incapable of showing where the Sex Purchase Act fails, and instead choose to question the motivation behind it.

The Norwegian Debate

We could never have imagined how strong the opposition to the Norwegian Sex Purchase Act would be when it was first implemented on January 1, 2009—by the police, who hardly enforce it; by politicians, who have made lifting the ban part of their election promises; and by the media, who are providing a platform for opponents of the act and for those who praise prostitution.

Again and again, articles reproduce the myth of "the world's oldest trade," "the happy hooker," and the prostitute as a "sex worker." In June 2013, Norway's largest newspaper, VG, presented the "sex worker" as an intelligent woman who has chosen everything herself.[124] She is safe and sound, her work is exciting and lucrative, there are no problems what-so-ever, and she can easily earn a lot of money! She practices good hygiene as well, and she dreams of future bliss with children and a faithful husband. What more can any sex buyer dream of, other than that once again it will be as legal to buy a woman as any other product?

The Politics: Leadership and Grassroots Movements

The Red/Green government coalition of 2005–2013 can at best be characterised as political paralysis, and at worst as downright sabotage of the Sex Purchase Act. It is no secret that the Sex Purchase Act was implemented against the will of the leaders of both the Labour Party and the Socialist Left Party. Minister of Justice at the time, Knut Storberget, was a strong opponent of the new act and the one who was set to implement it. Knowing this, it might not come as a surprise that the law has been enforced in a very lax manner. The result of this is that the situation in some cities and municipalities is about the same as before,

---

[123] *The Swedish Sex Purchase Act: Claimed Success and Documented Effects*, Östergren and Dodillet (2011), p. 25.
[124] *VG*, May 4, 2013.

whereas the situation in others has actually wo00rsened since the act's implementation.

Strip clubs and various "massage parlours" are now opening up in locations around the country. Advertising online is increasing, and trafficked women from Nigeria are a common sight on many Norwegian streets. The current situation, in which the purchase of sexual services is common and the police rarely interfere, creates contempt for the Sex Purchase Act and has led leading local politicians in Stavanger, one of Norway's largest cities, to claim that the act is ridiculous, and that it does not work. The front pages of newspapers scream about "the whore shock in Stavanger" and that "the whore traffic is back," while the role of procurers and sex buyers goes nearly unmentioned in the discussion. Several debaters are speaking up for banning not only the act of buying sexual services, but also selling.

This is in contrast to the position of many national politicians who wish to legalise prostitution. They are led by the "facts" presented by the Pro Centre, the Norwegian authority on prostitution, and research reports from Fafo, the unions' research institution. Most of the information on the Norwegian Sex Purchase Act that is spread internationally is coming from one of these two institutions. Because of this, it is important for the international public to know a little bit more about these two actors.

Ideological Research and Other Propaganda

Fafo is the Norwegian unions' research centre that mostly engages in research on labour and international solidarity. The sociologist May-Len Skilbrei has been a central part of Fafo's efforts to build up an academic environment within the organisation, where they also research the sex industry from a labour perspective. To Fafo prostitution is work, not violence.

All reports on stripping and prostitution coming from Fafo have a very clear political agenda. In 2009, only a few days after the act was implemented, May-Len Skilbrei concluded that the Sex Purchase Act had failed. She wrote a column for the newspaper Klassekampen in which she noted that the act was ineffective. Skilbrei is not the only researcher at Fafo who holds this opinion. During a panel discussion in 2008, Guri Tyldum at Fafo drew the same conclusion. But these researchers had arrived at their conclusion a long time before. Already in 2006, Guri Tyldum and May-Len Skilbrei, together with Anette Brunovskis, had concluded that the Swedish Sex Purchase Act had no effect, and thus should be overturned.[125]

In May 2013, Fafo presented a report entitled "Organisation, Conditions and Everyday Life in Norwegian Strip Clubs" that is representative of the kind of ideological "research" that has been conducted by them in the last five years. We will now take a closer look at this report, which was ordered by the Norwegian Ministry of Children, Equality, and Social Inclusion as part of a study on a possible ban on strip clubs, and was written by Ingunn Bjørkhaug, May-Len Skilbrei, and Kristin Alsos. Over a period of seven months, the researchers questioned 30 informants—both strippers and other participants—in the Norwegian strip industry. They concluded that the strippers are resourceful "dancers" who are not suffering any kind of exploitation; quite to the contrary, they make good money and live very well during their stay in Norway. The authors did not see any link between the strip clubs and prostitution.

The researchers at Fafo say they have not studied the strip clubs from a social perspective, and they have chosen not to ask about, or research in any other way, where the money from the strip clubs goes. When they also chose not to ask about or research how close the private dancers are to prostitution, what kind of individuals make up the customer base, which long-term effects the strippers experience, and what it means for those involved and those around them that women's bodies and sexuality are turned into sexual entertainment for men, it burdens their research with a major weakness. We know absolutely nothing more about Norwegian strip clubs since this report was presented. In addition to the above-mentioned weaknesses, the researchers continuously use politically charged language by which strippers are rewritten as "dancers" and facilitators are called "agents," and whereby the nomadic life of a stripper, because of the clients' demand for a constant

---

[125] *Aftenposten*, June 23, 2006.

stream of new women, is a consequence of tax conditions. All of these factors combine make the report a political document rather than a well-crafted piece of research.

The report "Experiences from Five Prostitution Measures During Six Months"[126] by Fafo's Anette Brunovskis continues on the same track. On page 35 the report describes how vulnerable women in prostitution are—not because they are exploited by procurers and customers, or because prostitution in general might be bad for them, but because the police are fighting the sex industry and arresting procurers and facilitators. And now the Sex Purchase Act is no longer the only law under attack. The Procuring Act, which is more than 100 years old and which makes profiting from other people's prostitution illegal, is being attacked. According to the report, violence against prostitutes in Oslo has spiked as a result of strong police enforcement of the Procuring Act, and the report concludes that the act thus should be "softened up." Brunovskis claims that not only should women be prostituted at the brothels; they should be able to live there, too. This gives Fafo's critique of the act an almost racist tone. Most prostitutes in Norway are not Norwegian but are rather trafficked in from poorer countries. Instead of suggesting the government come up with better assistance strategies to help those who want to leave prostitution, as well as measures such as housing, social benefits, and job placement assistance, the demand from this research institution is that the police should leave these women in peace at the brothels.

The Norwegian National Centre of Expertise: The Pro Centre

The Pro Centre is both a national authority on prostitution and a low-threshold centre for people in prostitution. Their role in spearheading the Norwegian pro-prostitution lobby is thoroughly documented in several chapters in this book, but judging from propaganda that we observe being spread internationally, we feel compelled to write something about their 2012 report, "Dangerous Liaisons, A Report on the Violence Prostitutes in Oslo Are Subjected To."[127]

---

[126] Fafo-rapport 2013:29.
[127] Farlige forbindelser, en rapport om volden kvinner i prostitusjon i Oslo utsettes for. Ulla Bjørndal (2012).

It is natural to assume that as a national centre of expertise, designed to be a governmental tool in this area, the Pro Centre would evaluate their priorities when the act that prohibits buying sexual services became law. But in this case, the institution continued on the same track as before. The Pro Centre does not seem to think it is their main task to help women leave prostitution, but rather to fight Norwegian legislation.

Ulla Bjørndahl at the Pro Centre delivered the "Dangerous Liaisons" report in June 2012. Several newspapers made room for this on their front pages, with the claim that "the Sex Purchasing Act is to blame," and the Conservative Party made it clear that they would start to work toward repealing the act. The headline declared that violence against prostitutes had increased after the act was implemented. The report had already been distributed to many countries as the truth about the Norwegian Sex Purchase Act, even before we were given the chance to read it and debunk it. The entire report is humbug and unscientific through and through. The Pro Centre was met with facts and arguments, and in Norway the report fell to the ground without making much of an impression on public opinion. It has, however, done much harm internationally. In many countries, "Dangerous Liaisons" is still portrayed as the truth about the Norwegian Sex Purchase Act.

What the report does show, however unintended, is that the Sex Purchase Act does, in fact, work. The report's own data tell us that the incidence of grave violence has been reduced since the act was implemented. On page 26 of the report, one reads that rape has declined by almost half, down from 29% of prostitutes to 15%; "hit by fist" has decreased from 29% to 18%; and "hit by flat hand" has gone down from 27% to 19%. The increased violence the Pro Centre was referring to turns out to be in the categories "groped," "called abusive names," "pulling hair," and "being spat at." Either way, this is a curious way of tabulating violence, as prostitution has always been violent. The report also explicitly states that the reason why prostitutes are displeased is that there are fewer customers, and thus poorer conditions for prostitution.[128]

---

[128] For a thorough analysis of the report, see Samantha Berg's exquisite blog post on Feministcurrent.com.

Iceland and the Porn Industry

Iceland went further than the other Nordic countries when it implemented the Sex Purchase Act by also shutting down the strip clubs. The workers in the clubs were mostly foreign women who moved from country to country. So-called "agents" cashed large sums every month from the women, whom they held under strict control, and saw to it that they behaved; otherwise their salaries would not be paid.

The main source of income for these women was the private dances, where nobody controlled what happened between the customer and the woman. The women's plane tickets and passports were taken from them, and they had to perform five free trial dances of the owners' choice, and also sign a contract binding them to absolute confidentiality. In addition, the women lived under the threat of sky-high fines for any small mistake, and their rent was five times higher than that of the public. The women were given minimum wages at the end of their contracted period, and the rest depended on how satisfied the club owners and agent were with the woman's behavior.

The porn industry is profitable, and a lot of creativity is required to get around the law. Recently three so-called champagne clubs have debuted in Reykjavik. The customers buy champagne for 20,000 Icelandic crowns—the same price as for a prostitute—and the price includes a private meeting with foreign women to have them sing or dance or have a chat, although many of the women speak neither Icelandic nor English.

The Sex Purchase Act in Iceland has, for the most part, gone unenforced. Since 2009 there has only been one conviction—of eight men who bought sex from the same woman. They were ordered to pay low fines, and the trial took place behind closed doors. In a TV interview, the leader of the police association stated that the act is so ambiguous and badly written that there is almost no point in trying to enforce it. Within the police force there is not a single officer who has been given the task of investigating prostitution. The important job of enforcing the act was given to the department that handles sexual abuse and which was already understaffed.

Judging from ads in newspapers and online, one can clearly see that the demand for prostitution is high. Nothing has been done to try to shut down the websites or to ban advertising in newspapers. After much pressure—and, most important, activism on the part of feminist groups—changes finally took place in 2011. The former Minister of Internal Affairs budgeted extra funding for the police group investigating organised crime to enable them to focus on prostitution. In 2013, the police report that they have investigated more than 100 cases, and these are now with the state attorney. Although there has been progress over the last two years, we must reluctantly conclude that there seems to be a lack of political will to enforce the act in Iceland, as in Norway.

Unlike the other Nordic countries, Iceland has no pro-prostitution organisations of their own, nor any public spokesperson opposing the act. None of the political parties work toward repealing the act, although it must be said that much more could have been done to enforce it.

A Ban on Buying Sex Works

Despite the fact that the Sex Purchase Act seems to have reduced the number of sex buyers and made Norway a less attractive country for traffickers, there is still much to criticise. Measures to help women find housing and work and to be recognised as victims of trafficking are still needed. A focus on sex buyers' use of violence is also crucial.

The polices' lack of enforcement, as well as the partial sabotage of the act, are important shortcomings, and the same can be said for the lack of cooperation among the police, social services, and voluntary organisations to offer the women in prostitution an alternative. The lack of an exit program is part of what we in the feminist movement see as sabotage of the act. The Sex Purchase Act in Norway has been shaky from the start, hampered by massive opposition from the support services for people in prostitution, research institutions, and politicians. Even so, the act functions so well that Norway's new right-wing government dreads its repeal before they can identify a strategy for avoiding opening up Norwegian back streets to the international mafia.

It is because of the act's tenuous position in Norway that the pro-prostitution lobby generally uses Norway as the example when they want to illustrate that the Sex Purchase Act doesn't work. But we believe that even though we don't yet have a society free of porn, prostitution, and trafficking, a ban on the purchase of sex is an important step along the way. As the Pro Centre's data show, serious violence against prostitutes has decreased markedly, and the prostitution market in most Norwegian cities and municipalities has weakened slightly since the implementation of the act. Because the Norwegian act will not be evaluated for a few years, we still don't know how it has affected the number of Norwegian men buying sex, nor do we have any such data from Iceland. Icelandic feminists are complaining that the police aren't doing enough to enforce the act, but they have no strong spokespersons working to repeal the ban, and Iceland has little contact with the international pro-prostitution lobby.

The political will to repeal the Sex Purchase Act in Sweden is close to non-existent, and Sweden has also taken it upon themselves to promote the Nordic model internationally. The Swedish police give priority to enforcing the act and also willingly participate in international conferences to showcase their important work and encourage other countries to follow their lead. The above-mentioned evaluation of the Sex Purchase Act and the active role of the government neutralises many of the undocumented claims from the pro-prostitution lobby.

The evaluation of the Sex Purchase Act shows that since its implementation, Sweden has become less attractive to organised crime. Street prostitution has been reduced by 50%, and fewer men now buy sex. In the same way that the common Nordic ban on physical punishment of children has led to a collective awareness among Nordic parents that hitting children is unacceptable, the Sex Purchase Act has led to an increased awareness among Nordic men that buying sexual services is inherently wrong.

According to Interpol, illegal trafficking alone brings in around €11 billion yearly. Both Swedish and Norwegian police believe that the Sex Purchase Act is a good tool for fighting organised crime. The act expedites their ability to intervene in brothels and to wage the battle against human traffickers and the prostitution of minors.

We are fighting a patriarchal system, and a ban on the purchase of sexual services challenges the prevailing gender order. The Sex Purchase Act is part of a struggle against structures and attitudes that reduce women and our sexuality to a product, and it establishes the fact that prostitution is about the society's attitude toward women, social development, and gender equality. The Nordic model is an alternative to treating prostitution with a conservative double standard, that is, seeing it as a problem of public order, and to relegating the trade in humans to certain parts of town. The act is also unique in that it acknowledges the unequal power balance between supply and demand.

Many countries impose a ban on both buying and selling sexual services, but the sole result is that prostitutes become more helpless and lose yet more legal protection. Men being bothered by desperate and aggressive prostitutes can be a problem, but criminalising the victims of human trafficking is not the solution. A ban on selling sexual services affects those who are already victims. This knowledge is the basis for the choice to ban purchasing of sexual services, not the sale of them, as reflected in the Sex Purchase Act implemented in Sweden, Norway, and Iceland. The Nordic model stands in solidarity with all women, and it is based on human rights and the knowledge that prostitution is violence against women.

The Nordic model changes men's attitudes and actions and is thus an essential measure for ending prostitution. But an act alone is not enough. For the act to have its intended effect, the police need to enforce it, and it is critical that it be followed up by various measures to help the women in prostitution and to strengthen awareness campaigns directed toward men. In addition, the society as a whole needs to support the idea that women are not for sale. Prostitution and human trafficking are billion-Euro international industries, but they can be stopped if more countries follow the lead of Sweden, Norway, and Iceland, and discourage men from feeding the monster by buying the goods the industry offers.

www.ingramcontent.com/pod-product-compliance
Lightning Source LLC
Chambersburg PA
CBHW070422290526
45791CB00005B/1790